YORK HAN

GENERAL EDITOR:
Professor A.N. Jeffares
(*University of Stirling*)

STUDYING THE BRONTËS

Sheila Sullivan
MA (OXFORD)

LONGMAN
YORK PRESS

Plates 1, 3 and 5 are reproduced by courtesy of the Mansell Collection.

Plate 2 is reproduced by courtesy of the Brontë Society.

Plate 4 is reproduced by courtesy of the National Portrait Gallery.

YORK PRESS
Immeuble Esseily, Place Riad Solh, Beirut.

LONGMAN GROUP UK LIMITED
Longman House, Burnt Mill, Harlow,
Essex CM20 2JE, England
and Associated Companies throughout the World.

First published 1986

ISBN 0-582-96600-0

Produced by Longman Group (FE) Ltd
Printed in Hong Kong

Contents

PLATES

Part 1

The Brontës and their world

Historical background

Events

Patrick Brontë and his surviving children lived under the reigns of George III, George IV, William IV and Victoria. This first fifty years of the nineteenth century was a period of upheaval and reform. In politics, the two great parties of Whig and Tory, together with the new Radicals, initiated far-reaching changes. The Reform Bill of 1832 re-organised constituencies and reduced corruption in the Parliamentary system. In the Church, the final acceptance of Methodists and other Dissenters, who belonged to religious bodies outside the Church of England, marked a new tolerance; the Catholic Emancipation Act of 1829 allowed Catholics to join in political and public life, and the Marriage Act of 1836 permitted Catholics and Dissenters to marry in churches and chapels of their own faiths. The beginnings of serious social reform had their roots in this time; acts abolishing slavery, re-forming the Poor Laws, allowing the formation of Trades Unions, and limiting the hours of factory work, were among many passed in these fifty years.

The Duke of Wellington defeated Napoleon at Waterloo in 1815. For many years there had been a strong anti-war party, because (as Moore finds in *Shirley*) the war ruinously restricted trade. But at last the long war with France came to an end, and the problems of the peace began, in great social and political unrest (see below). Through their father, with his passionate interest in military, political, and religious matters, the Brontë children became aware very young of this stirring of new ideas. Of their seven published novels, only *Shirley* deals directly with political agitation and Dissent, but the juvenile writing of Charlotte and Branwell, in particular, was fed with tales of the exploits of the Duke of Wellington, their father's hero, and the model for Charlotte's King of Angria. Their adult works are much concerned with many of the preoccupations of the day, especially social problems of marriage, wealth and class. Charlotte and Anne are particularly biting

in their portraits of leisured, wealthy women, such as the Ingrams (JE)*
and the Bloomfields (AG), who think only of marriage and money and
fashion.

Poverty and unrest

The rapid growth in population, and the abrupt fall in prices after the
war, brought widespread unemployment and poverty. Added to this,
the growth of large estates, such as Rochester's (JE) and the Lintons'
(WH), reduced the number of small farms, and the new tenant farmers
could pay their labourers only the barest wage. In the North, a rapid in-
crease in the number of iron-works, and of wool and cotton mills, re-
sulted in the collapse of the old village trades and crafts. Poverty was
further increased by the Corn Law of 1815, which held the price of
bread at a level the poor could not meet. In the mills and mines women
and children worked unlimited hours, and returned home to the first
industrial slums. In both town and country the unemployed poor, or
'paupers', were barely kept alive by public funds. The Brontës saw
poverty and destitution in plenty in their own village of Haworth, and
in the surrounding countryside. In their novels they express a genuine
sympathy, and scorn the condescending charity of the rich; Agnes Grey
prefers to visit the cottagers on her own, without the patronising company of the Murray girls; the young Jane Eyre expresses her horror of
poverty to the apothecary; and Caroline (Sh) urges Moore to be more
compassionate.

A sharp sense of social injustice among the poor and unemployed
created unrest and rioting. In 1811–12 Yorkshire and Midlands
saw the first 'Luddite' riots, called after Ned Ludd, against the introduction of the new power-driven machinery, which deprived the hand-
weavers of their livelihoods. Patrick Brontë witnessed rioting in 1811,
when he was the minister at Hartshead, and he took to carrying pistols
to protect the property of his parishioners – a practice gently satirised
by Charlotte in her portait of Helstone in *Shirley*. Indeed, Brontë lived
the rest of his life in fear of Luddites, practised pistol-shooting daily,
and never walked unarmed. The Luddites did not object only to the
new machinery: they also demanded some regulation of wages and
hours of work. The most notorious of the Luddite attacks was that on
Cartwright's mill at Rawfold in 1811, when rioters attacked with
muskets and axes. It is this incident which forms the basis of the attack
on Moore's mill in *Shirley*, and Moore's character probably owes

* In this handbook the following abbreviations will be used to denote works by the
Brontës when cited as references: AG (*Agnes Grey*), JE (*Jane Eyre*), P (*The Professor*),
Sh (*Shirley*), TWH (*The Tenant of Wildfell Hall*), V (*Villette*), WH (*Wuthering Heights*).

something to that of Cartwright. In 1815, in protest at the Corn Law, there was more rioting and burning of haystacks and ricks. The penalties were fierce, often including hanging or transportation for life to Australia. Then in 1819 a crowd from the mills in Manchester, meeting on St Peter's Fields to demand parliamentary reform, was charged by soldiers and some dozen people were killed. The confrontation became known as 'Peterloo' (or the Peterloo Massacre), and it did much to disturb the public conscience.

Reform

By the 1820s the cause of reform was stirring, greatly encouraged by the new Radical party and the conscience of the Dissenters. The first Mechanics' Institute was founded in 1823, for encouraging learning among ill-educated adults. It was from the library of the Institute at nearby Keighley that Patrick borrowed books to help to meet the voracious reading appetite of his young family. Trades associations, or unions, were first permitted in 1828, although they were limited in their power. In 1832 came the first Reform Bill, which cleared some of the corruption surrounding parliamentary elections. In 1833 slavery (which had been abolished as a trade in 1807) was now forbidden as a practice throughout Britain's colonies, and in the same year a new Poor Law established 'workhouses', where the old, the sick, and the needy were given spartan shelter. The Factory Act of 1833 limited the working hours of children, and in 1846 the hated Corn Laws were repealed, allowing the import of cheap foreign grain and so lowering the high price of bread. The Mines Act of 1842 forbade the underground employment of women, and of children under ten, in the mines, and the Ten Hours Act of 1844 limited the working day of women and children in textile mills.

The position of women

Women did not have the vote, or any share in political life. They could inherit family money and estates if there were no brothers, but as soon as they became 'heiresses' they were pursued unscrupulously. Even Robert Moore is not above seeking out Shirley for her money (Sh). Before the Married Women's Property Act (1882) a married woman's wealth became her husband's on marriage. So, like Helen Huntingdon (TWH), she was very much at her husband's mercy.

The place of women in society was central to the concerns of Charlotte and, to a lesser extent, of Anne. Charlotte thought and wrote much on the matter (see 'Charlotte Brontë: Writings' pp.32–40). Although they apparently did not resent the money set aside for

Branwell's education, the girls were indignant at the obstacles put in the path of able women, especially of those who were unmarried and needed to earn a living. At that time (and for many years to come) there were no professions open to women, except teaching; they could not be doctors, lawyers, politicians or administrators, or indeed anything much except teachers, actresses, servants, mill hands – or authors. The Brontës took up two of the professions that were open to them, and became teachers and authors, but both for themselves and for others, they felt the frustration of clever women whose outlets were so severely limited.

They had a good education themselves, both at home and at school, and they considered education vitally necessary for girls, who, they thought, should be brought up, like their brothers, in habits of independence and hard work. Most girls of the middle and upper classes were only skimpily educated, if at all. 'Accomplishments', such as music, drawing, and sewing were considered necessary, but many girls would never acquire more than a smattering of any intellectual subject. Most, like the Murrays (AG) and the Ingrams (JE), aimed to make a wealthy marriage, and if they failed were likely to become lonely, poor and despised. The Misses Ainley and Mann are two touching examples provided by Charlotte (Sh). The Brontës believed that if a woman was educated, and she could not marry happily, then she need not make a mercenary marriage, nor need she remain an idle and dispirited spinster at home. Charlotte greatly admired women who had the courage to make their own way. Only thus, she thought, could the unmarried find a worthy purpose in the world.

Girls from poor homes could become little other than domestic servants. If they were fortunate, they might be as happy as Tabitha Ackroyd appears to have been in the Brontës' own household; but many were not fortunate at all. In the first quarter of the nineteenth century women employed as servants still far outnumbered those employed in the mills, and their wages were so low that even humble households could afford to employ them. The Brontës seem to have been fortunate in all their servants; Tabby was a loved member of the parsonage for many years, and aspects of her brisk, kindly character appear in many of the Brontës fictional servants, such as Nelly Dean (WH), Rachel (TWH), and Bessie and Hannah (JE).

Health

In order to write, or do anything else, one first had to stay alive. And in the first half of the nineteenth century, when sanitation, public health and medical knowledge were still rudimentary, staying alive was no mean feat. By the end of the eighteenth century the death-rate was falling, but between about 1810 and 1850 it ceased to fall at all, largely because of the rapid spread of disease in the crowded new slums. Tuberculosis, smallpox, cholera, typhus, dysentery and unidentified 'fevers' were familiar terrors, and often fatal. Many of the symptoms of disease were well documented, but the way in which it spread was barely understood; the effect of contaminated water, of lice and flies, of tubercular milk, of malnutrition, and of crowded conditions was only slowly appreciated. Seepage from earth closets, open drains and drinking water ran side by side, often merging into each other. At Haworth the village drinking supply ran through the graveyard before it reached the village wells. Indeed, the death-rate at Haworth was so high that in 1850 an official enquiry was established. It reported that the average age at the time of death was twenty-five years, and that 41% of the population died before they were six. Lice were prevalent even in clean and respectable homes, where they were recognised as a nuisance but not as carriers of the dreaded typhus; Charlotte assumes that the typhus of Lowood (JE) was a 'fog-bred pestilence'. Nor was it realised that flies as well as water were transmitters of cholera. Hospitals were few and primitive, and home medical care was supplied by apothecaries, such as Mr Lloyd (JE), and by doctors like Graham Bretton (V), who still prescribed 'bleeding' with leeches, and often had to ride many miles over muddy tracks to their patients. Although illness does not play a major part in the Brontës' novels, both Helen Burns (JE) and Frances Earnshaw (WH) die of tuberculosis, a disease which devastated the Brontë family. Maria, Elizabeth, Emily and Anne all died of it, and it was probably implicated in Branwell's death also. Their mother died of cancer when Charlotte was only five, and most of the heroines of the novels have lost their mothers.

Travel

The roads of England were still often no more than tracks, thinly surfaced and deeply rutted by the wheels of carts and horse-drawn coaches. People on foot (as most people were) made constant use of rough paths across fields and hills, as they do in the Brontës' novels; Caroline and Shirley (Sh) walk constantly, and as a matter of course, through fields and woods. Long-distance journeys by stage-coach (such as that made by Branwell to London in 1835) were gradually replaced by rail-travel during the Brontës' life-time. The first railways were built in the 1820s, and the network was rapidly developed, until by the middle of the century most major cities and towns were served. The Brontës began to do their own modest travelling by train in the 1840s, and in 1840 Branwell was appointed railway-clerk at

PLATE 1: The Parsonage and graveyard at Haworth, c. 1856.

Sowerby Bridge, and later station-master at Luddenham Foot. However, none of the characters in any of the novels makes a journey by train.

Home and family

The Yorkshire moors, Haworth parsonage, and their close-knit family life, were all of deep significance in the lives and works of the Brontës. They moved to Haworth in 1820, when Charlotte was four, and it was home for all of them throughout their short lives. The year after they moved their mother died, and none of her three author-daughters could afterwards remember her. Her death must have had a profound effect, made even more terrible by the deaths of the two older girls, Maria and Elizabeth, in 1825.

The square grey parsonage still stands at the top of the steep village street, with church and churchyard beside it. Beyond, for miles in all directions, are the moors. These windy uplands, deeply cut with streams and gullies, covered with heather and rocks and stunted trees, became a playground for the four adventurous children. Led chiefly by Emily, they came to know the rocks and dells, animals and flowers, and the moors became one of the great stimulants of their creativity. Not only are they are a frequent background in the novels, they became a symbolic embodiment of elemental forces.

The parsonage itself was not a cheerful-looking place. Mrs Gaskell (1810–65), who in 1857 published the first biography of Charlotte, found it dreary, and 'literally paved with rain-blackened tombstones'. Yet within it the family was close and happy for many years; as children they yelled and tumbled until their servant Tabby thought they were 'all going mad'. It was not until the final failure of Branwell in the mid-1840s that distress and some dissension disturbed their family life. The girls seem to have felt that their family duties were even more important than their writing; Emily made delicious bread and learned German grammar at the same time. And in spite of their spirited belief in the independence of women, they accepted that Branwell was privileged, and they must help their father to support him.

Whenever they departed from home, as pupils to school, and later as teachers or governesses, they longed to return. With Anne's help, Emily kept occasional 'diary-papers', written in a brisk, racy prose, which relate the small events and conversations of the day. These tell much about the affectionate, teasing, busy life of the family, and reveal the endearing, muddled way in which bed-making, writing, potato-peeling, lessons, piano-practice, and more writing were all intermingled. There were few of the amenities now thought necessary for comfortable living. Lighting was by oil-lamps and candles, heat came from the kitchen-range, and sometimes a fire in dining-room or study. When Mrs Gaskell came to visit in 1853 she noticed bright fires in every room—but by then Charlotte and her father were comparatively prosperous. Because of Patrick's terror of fire there were no curtains in the house, and buckets of water stood in the hall.

The six Brontë children were born within six years, and the four survivors between 1816 and 1820, so the age differences were slight. Although each had his or her distinctive outlook, there was an unusual unity of thought and feeling among them. In 1841 Charlotte wrote of the deep affection brothers and sisters feel for each other 'when their minds are cast in the same mould'. So much is this evident in the work of the sisters, that the first reviewers of the first published novels assumed the authors were brothers, or even one person.

To southerners at the beginning of the last century Yorkshire seemed a remote, barbaric region of desolate landscape and dirty mill-towns. In her Preface to the 1850 edition of *Wuthering Heights*, Charlotte acknowledges Yorkshire's 'unintelligible and even repulsive reputation', and Mrs Gaskell did little to soften the outlines. Haworth was as wild and remote as anywhere. Apart from a few of their father's parishioners, and his succession of curates, the Brontës had little outside social life. As he became older, Branwell found company for drinking and gambling, but the girls were isolated. They do not seem to have minded (although Charlotte came to resent the narrowness of her circle) and they never became accustomed to the sophisticated behaviour expected by their wealthier and more fashionable friends. After the success of *Jane Eyre* Charlotte made several visits to London, but she never learned to overcome her awkward shyness.

The young Brontës, however, were by no means cut off from the events and ideas of the time. Their father saw to this. He was born in Ireland, the son of an Irish labourer (who spelled his name Brunty), and he bequeathed a touch of his Irish accent to his children. By his own efforts he won a place at Cambridge, and was eventually ordained. He was fervently interested in politics, warfare, and affairs of state; indeed he probably missed his true vocation as soldier or politician because of his poverty at Cambridge—certainly Charlotte thought so. He shared his enthusiasms with his children, and provided them with political and literary journals, of which their favourite was *Blackwood's Magazine* (see 'Unpublished writings', pp.23−6). He supplied them with books from the library of the Mechanics' Institute, and gave them the freedom of his own large and varied collection. The children became familiar with the Bible, the *Arabian Nights*, the works of Shakespeare, Bunyan, Milton, Defoe, Johnson, Scott, the Romantic poets, and many works of travel, history, biography and natural history. Patrick was himself a published author of poems and stories, and he understood the pleasure of writing. This was just as well, because before his four scribbling children reached their teens they were writing, in Emily's words, 'from morning till noon, and from noon till night', sometimes two thousand words a day.

Although the children were sent briefly to school at various times, they were chiefly educated by their father at home. Among various subjects, he taught them classics, English literature, history and geography, and engaged an art-master for Branwell and a music teacher for the girls. He was in some ways eccentric, and sometimes explosive, and he had a puritanical suspicion of cards, dancing, and the theatre; yet he seems to have been a tolerant and encouraging father, and a devoted, hard-working parson.

Aunt Branwell, his wife's unmarried sister, came to look after the children just before their mother died, and she lived with them until her death over twenty years later. She seems to have been an intelligent, positive woman, capable of confronting her brother-in-law and of holding her own in the remarkable family in which she found herself. She was a Methodist, and she has sometimes been blamed for causing the religious fears undergone by Anne, but it seems unlikely that Patrick would have allowed fanatical beliefs to distress his children; and indeed Charlotte learned to laugh at her 'mad Methodist Magazines'.

The children seem to have spent much of their free time with their much-loved servant Tabby in the warm kitchen. Her stories of the old days, when the valley-bottoms were filled with fairies instead of mills, must have excited the children's interest in the supernatural, which was to play a significant part in the adult work of Charlotte and Emily.

Their own childhood does not seem to be closely reflected in their novels, although there is probably something of Emily in Catherine Earnshaw's (WH) love of the moors, and Emily's poems are full of visions of lost happiness. Children receive varied treatment in the novels. None of the Brontës was sentimental on the subject, and of course none ever had a child of her own (Charlotte died in pregnancy). All of them portray children who are cruel, over-indulged, and ill-disciplined. The Reeds (JE) and the Bloomfields (AG) are the type of odious children both Charlotte and Anne encountered in their careers as governesses. Noticeably, they are the children of the kind of rich, lazy women the Brontës despised. The appealing children in the novels —Jane Eyre, Matthew Yorke (Sh), Catherine Linton (WH) and Polly (V)—are spirited, honest, and affectionate.

Branwell Brontë (1817–1848)

Although Branwell published nothing, and died when he was only thirty-one of drink, drugs, and possibly tuberculosis, he was very much a part of his sisters' lives and their work. He was the only boy in a family of six, and his sisters seem to have acknowledged that he should be privileged. They did not resent that he was destined for an expensive course as an art student in London, and they felt it their duty to take up posts as teachers and governesses to help their father with the fees.

After the deaths of Maria and Elizabeth in 1825, Branwell became very close to Charlotte, and she to him. Their literary invention and production was prodigious. No doubt Charlotte would have written without him, but whether she would have found such a vehicle for her fantasy as the Young Men, Glass Town and Angria (see 'Unpublished writings' pp.23–6) no-one can know. Branwell's toy soldiers, given him by his father in 1826, seem to have instigated the 'plays', which led to the four islands of the Glass Town saga.

Branwell was an excitable, precocious boy with ginger hair. After his death Charlotte described him as the best-looking of the family, but surviving portraits do not seem to bear this out. He was greatly beloved by his sisters, a favourite of Aunt Branwell, and in his early youth the apple of his father's eye. He was chiefly educated at home, where his father taught him a wide range of subjects, and he read voraciously. When he was twelve, he and Charlotte made up the first of their miniscule booklets imitating *Blackwood's Magazine*. He wrote verse and prose with equal facility, but he did more than write; he was the most talented, in a highly talented family, at drawing and painting. His proud and indulgent father engaged an art teacher to help him, and to ensure that he would be accepted by the Academy Schools in London. But Branwell was already finding his amusements outside the parsonage, in public houses and the local boxing-club.

In 1835 he set off to join the Academy Schools, but he never presented his letters of introduction, spent his money in a pub, and returned home saying he had been robbed. He sent brash and conceited letters, urging the excellence of his own writing, both to *Blackwood's* and to the poet William Wordsworth (1770–1850), but received no replies. In 1838 his father set him up as a portrait painter in Bradford, but the next year he was home again, drinking heavily and probably taking drugs. With touching faith, his family still believed he might fulfil his promise. In 1839 he went to a private family as a tutor, but he was dismissed after six months, and became a clerk at the new railway-station at Sowerby Bridge. In 1841 he was promoted to station-master at Luddenden Foot, but his accounts were found to be irregular and in 1842 he was dismissed. Deeply distressed and ashamed, he sank further

into depression and drank heavily. Anne came to his rescue by per-
suading her employers, the Robinsons, to take him on as tutor to their
son. He embarked on a long and complex relationship with Mrs Robinson, with whom he evidently fell in love, and was dismissed by her
exasperated husband in 1845. His own version of the story is told in the
unfinished Angrian fragment, *And the Weary are at Rest*.

By now his family's loyalty was strained to breaking-point. Charlotte and Anne despaired, and even Emily, his most staunch defender,
now thought him 'hopeless'. He died in September 1848, of the effects
of alcohol and opium, and probably tuberculosis as well.

His tragically wasted life is of no importance to literature or painting, but it had a deep effect on the feelings of his sisters, who had loved
and admired him. His history was directly responsible, on Anne's own
account, for her determination to write *The Tenant of Wildfell Hall*.
Hindley's drinking in *Wuthering Heights*, and some of Emily's poems
(especially 'The Wanderer from the Fold') no doubt derive something
from Branwell's life.

Religion and the Church

Patrick Brontë was ordained into the Church of England in 1807. The
religious revival known as Methodism was firmly established by John
Wesley (1703–91) towards the end of the eighteenth century. His
influence was widespread and deep. Not only did it stimulate the older
dissenting sects, such as the Quakers and the Baptists, but by the turn
of the century its innumerable converts (drawn in great numbers from
the poor) had succeeded in arousing the Church of England from its
complacency, and provoking a ferment in religious life. The robust
hunting parson, more concerned with his pleasures than with his
parishioners, was often now succeeded by a more conscientious man,
influenced by the beliefs of the new Dissenters. Faith was seen as best
demonstrated in piety and good works, and faith in Christ brought
rebirth, the hope of salvation, and power over sin. Those upholding a
more extreme belief, the followers of John Calvin (1509–64), believed
in eternal damnation for the unrepentant; Emily described a man of
such beliefs in Joseph (WH), and Charlotte in Moses Barraclough (Sh).
Some critics of the Brontës believe that Branwell and Anne in
particular were deeply disturbed by these extreme beliefs, and for a
brief period at Roe Head Charlotte too felt the terror of the damned,
outcast from God.

Patrick was an 'evangelical', meaning that although he was a
devoted parson of the Church of England he sympathised with the
Methodists in their emphasis on piety and virtuous action. He was
tolerant of their chapels, and of many of their beliefs, and he and his

kind did much to bridge the awkward gap between the Dissenters and the orthodox church. His sister-in-law, the children's Aunt Branwell, was a convinced Methodist, but her views do not seem to have been so extreme that they became an irritant in the parsonage.

Methodism was especially popular among the working poor of the Industrial Revolution, and was often associated with political agitation. Many of the great reformers, such as the Earl of Shaftesbury (1801–85), were associated with Dissent. However, the growing link between Dissent and social unrest was not welcome at Patrick's High Tory parsonage. The ranting Methodist Barraclough (Sh) is also an agitator for Luddite violence (see 'Historical background' pp. 5–11 above).

Roman Catholicism was detested by Patrick, and in both *Shirley* and *Villette* Charlotte makes plain that she shares his feelings. Both were also scathing in their attitude to the new 'Puseyites', the Anglican followers of Dr Pusey (1800–82), who based much of their belief and practice on that of the Church of Rome. Part of her father's objection to Charlotte's engagement to his curate Mr Nicholls was based on his dislike of Nicholl's Puseyism. In a letter from Belgium in 1842, Charlotte wrote, 'I consider Methodism, Dissenterism, Quakerism, and the extremes of high and low Churchism foolish but Roman Catholicism beats them all'. But the Brontës were critical of their own church too. Charlotte's portrait of 'the shower of curates' in *Shirley* reveals her contempt for clerics who talk about minor matters of theology instead of tending their flocks; and Anne's satirical portrait of the contemptible Mr Hatfield (AG) shows how far she was from complacent acceptance of her own church. In approving a high-minded piety, backed by compassion and good deeds, the Brontës clearly felt they held the proper middle ground.

Religious belief, and worship at church and chapel, pervaded people's lives in a way unimaginable today, and the Brontë household was no exception. None of them seem ever to have seriously questioned the beliefs of the Anglican church, although Emily's feelings were not bound by strict creed or orthodoxy, and Charlotte's Jane Eyre briefly finds difficulty in praying. She is also troubled, as are Lucy Snowe (V) and Agnes Grey, in reconciling their love for men with their love for God.

The Brontës apparently believed, as did most people, that the appalling toll of sickness and death must be accepted with resignation as the mysterious will of God. In a letter written after the deaths of her brother and both her sisters, Charlotte asserts that these terrible events in no way shook her faith in divine wisdom. The beauty of the world was seen as a manifestation of God, and unusual events as signs of his approval or anger; when the children were young, their father told them that the remarkable eruption of a moorland bog was an act of Divine Wisdom. Atheism they despised; although Charlotte admired her friend Harriet Martineau (1802–76), she felt that no-one should trust an atheist.

Because Sunday was the only day of rest for working people, the church was a vital social meeting-place. Caroline (Sh), when forbidden to visit Moore, can see him only at church, and only at church does Agnes (AG) see Weston. Many people would attend church twice a day, as did the girls from Lowood (JE), who ate lunch between services in a room over the porch. The number of clerics who appear in the novels of Charlotte and Anne reflect this pervasive background of Anglican practice and belief.

The Bible was the first book most children knew, and as they grew up their knowledge became a part of their thoughts and feelings. The educated read it for themselves, or members of a family read it to each other, and the many who could not read heard it from the mouths of preachers and at church services. Its influence (greatly strengthened by the rise of Methodism) spread through all walks of life, and allusions to its stories would be understood by everyone. Phrases and allusions appear effortlessly and naturally throughout the writings of the Brontës, and particularly in Charlotte's work.

Love and marriage

No-one knows if Emily ever fell in love, but Anne loved one of her father's curates, William Weightman, and Charlotte fell deeply and unhappily in love with M. Heger, the husband of the headmistress of her Brussels school (see Charlotte's life, pp. 27–31). But whatever their own limited experience in real life, the Brontës wrote more on love than on any other subject, and they all understood the feelings of those in love. They began to exhibit this interest when they were still children; the tales of Glass Town, Angria and Gondal (see 'Unpublished writings', pp. 23–6) are filled with men and women entangled in romance and passion, and the later sections do not all read like immature fantasy. Emily's Gondal poem 'Cold in the Earth' is an eloquent lament for lost love, and Charlotte's later Angrian stories, such as 'Captain Henry Hastings' show the beginnings of an adult understanding of love.

Some of the early critics of their work remarked on the emphasis on love, especially in the lives of the heroines. Harriet Martineau, writing on *Villette* in 1853, considered that Charlotte's women were too dominated by the search for love. Even if this is not entirely just, it is true that Charlotte does not question the power of love, and its part in the creation of joy and pain. Charlotte and Anne seem driven to write of women alone and friendless, often in hopeless situations, and greatly in need of love. It is tempting to see something of their own childhood background in this search; none of them remembered their mother, and all suffered greatly from the death of their two older sisters.

Between them, they wrote of love in many aspects. The obsessive passion of Heathcliff for Cathy (WH) leads him to act with cruel savagery, and her sense of absolute identity with him leads to her death. There is an almost religious intensity in some of their words to each other, and in the hints of their life together beyond the physical world. Jane Eyre is afraid she will love Rochester to idolatry, as if he were God (just as the young Charlotte was afraid she would love her schoolfriend, Ellen Nussey). The fear is not uncommon in Brontë heroines; Lucy Snow (V) shares it, and so does Agnes Grey.

But not all Brontë characters love on this scale. The sisters were aware that love comes in degrees of intensity, and may be subtly modified by circumstances or by character. The loves of Catherine and Hareton, of Agnes Grey and Mr Weston, of Lucy and M. Paul, are seen as no less durable but rather less tumultuous than, say, Heathcliff's. In contrasting the passions of the two generations in *Wuthering Heights* Emily does not imply that the gentler feelings of the younger ones are any less valuable than the desperate loves of their elders; they are not cruel and disruptive emotions, but harmonious and full of hope. Other Brontë characters, such as Lockwood (WH), love feebly and without conviction; others again, such as Blanche Ingram (JE) and Rosalie Murray (AG), do not love at all but merely pretend, in order to achieve marriage and wealth. But whatever kind of love they are describing all the Brontës find its origins a mystery; as with Mr Yorke (Sh), 'somehow, for some reason... he loved her'.

The dictates of reason and the impulses of passion are held in constant tension in their books. Rochester's (JE) observation on Jane points the matter neatly: 'Reason sits firm and holds the reins... The passions may rage... but judgement shall still have the last word'. With the exception of Cathy and Heathcliff, who care nothing for judgement and reason, all the main protagonists have to find this balance somewhere. Charlotte's own views are openly revealed in her letters. In her early twenties, when she received the first of her four proposals of marriage, she felt it was necessary to adore and be ready to die for one's husband. But soon she came to take a more realistic view, and to regard mutual respect as a better basis for marriage than a grand passion. Shirley considers kindness the most important quality in a husband, and believes passion to be 'a mere fire of dry sticks'. And Anne finds the best basis for marriage in good sense, integrity, kindness, and cheerfulness (TWH). Love in these novels is usually strong enough to sweep away the barriers of class, wealth and religion. The wealthy Rochester wished to marry the humble Jane long before she acquired her fortune; Gilbert Markham (TWH) is held back by Helen's riches; and Shirley had to quell Louis Moore's awe of her wealth and rank.

The erotic aspects of love could not be discussed in the early nineteenth century. The public was readily shocked, and Charlotte was much distressed by some of the attacks on *Jane Eyre*. To us, the words she uses seem no more than honest and factual, but her public found them 'coarse'. Never again was she so frank about physical attraction. The erotic aspects of Rochester's masculinity, the intensity of Jane's agitation, or Rivers's temptation by Rosamond, are not repeated with later heroes and heroines, however much they may be implied. Nor did Anne escape censure. Although her references to Huntingdon's orgies are only oblique, she was severely treated by some reviewers. And Emily's crudity in *Wuthering Heights* was described as disgusting. She partly side-stepped this problem of propriety by presenting Cathy's feeling for Heathcliff as almost entirely asexual, even though rooted in her being. Heathcliff's feelings, however, are plain enough, and his jealousy is not glossed over. From the moment of his return, he is tormentingly jealous of Edgar, and Cathy's betrayal becomes the chief motive of his revenge. Angry male jealousy has little place in Charlotte's work, but Anne forcefully demonstrates its power in Markham (TWH). The jealousies suffered by women are painfully conveyed in *Villette*, in Lucy's anguish over Bretton, and in her discovery of Justine Marie, and Helen too (TWH) is made miserable by her husband's flirtation with Annabella. Jane Eyre, however, cannot feel jealous of Blanche Ingram because she despises her, and Caroline (Sh) cannot feel jealous of Shirley because she loves her.

The exultation of love is vividly expressed in *Jane Eyre*, especially in the summer garden when Jane declares herself; Helen's infatuation with Huntingdon (TWH) and Isabella's with Heathcliff (WH) briefly share this excitement. But it is rarely expressed in any of the other novels. The loves of the other heroines, such as Frances (P), Agnes (AG), Caroline (Sh) and Lucy (V), emerge from such pain that although they are profound they lack dizzy rapture. It is true that Cathy and Heathcliff share an idyllic happiness in childhood, but this does not develop into a normal adult love. And Shirley's love for Louis (Sh) is pitched so low it barely carries conviction.

Few of the Brontë heroines are good-looking; of Charlotte's only Shirley and Caroline (Sh) can claim beauty. Jane Eyre is acutely aware of her plain face, and she is also frightened by the confident good looks of others. Lucy Snowe (V) is also homely in appearance, with no confidence in her looks or charm. This is deliberate on Charlotte's part; she wished to have no hand in the kind of sentimental romance, popular in her day, which was filled with sultry Byronic heroes and ravishing women. Mrs

Gaskell assures us that Charlotte was small, and also plain (although the portraits do not seem to bear this out). Whatever the precise truth of the matter, none of the Brontës was a beauty, and both Charlotte and Anne seem to have put something of their own diffidence into their heroines. Both are sharply aware of the importance of looks in the game of love and marriage.

Right behaviour is important to all the Brontë heroines, except for Cathy (WH). None of them question the conventional morality of the time, and apart from Rochester's intent to deceive (JE), none of the men press them beyond the accepted limits. Elopement and adultery are not themes the Brontës pursued at any length, although Anne faces them in *The Tenant of Wildfell Hall*. Improper conduct between the sexes is always deplored, and its immorality never questioned. Jane's longing for Rochester is clearly expressed, as is that of Rivers for Rosamond (JE), but the feeling is restrained, as both Jane and Rivers believe it should be.

What is never questioned in these novels is the deep and disruptive power of love. Whether it is joyful and exultant, or whether it is bitter and unrequited, it is presented as the greatest emotional force which men and women have to face. Lucy Snowe's love for Paul Emanuel (V) sustains her even through the pain of his death, and Cathy's reaches out to Heathcliff beyond the grave. But how love relates to marriage is another matter. Most of the heroines' love-stories end happily, with the assumption that married happiness will be fulfilling and abiding, but this does not entirely reflect the Brontës' general view of marriage. All of them see marriage as a precarious venture, often deeply unhappy; Helen's first marriage (TWH) is a disaster, as are most of the marriages in *Wuthering Heights*. And in *Shirley* not one of the long-established marriages (Helstone's, Mrs Pryor's, the Yorkes') is presented as happy.

In the nineteenth century it was assumed that the greatest possible misfortune for a woman was not to marry. Charlotte in particular fought against this belief. Perhaps assuming, after her own blighted love for M. Heger, that she would never marry, she determined to show that a woman could live better single than trapped in a marriage made only for wealth and security. She told her old headmistress, Miss Wooler, that there was no character more respectable than a single woman who made her own way 'quietly, perseveringly'. It was then assumed, and taken as reasonable, that both men and women frequently married for money. Before the Married Women's Property Act of 1882 all a woman owned passed to her husband when she married, and the search for an heiress was a constant theme of novels from Samuel Richardson (1689–1761) onwards. Robert Moore plans to marry Shirley for her money (Sh), Cathy marries Edgar Linton for wealth and social prestige (WH), and Rochester is sent as a young man to the West Indies to capture Bertha Mason's fortune (JE).

Divorce was almost unknown in the nineteenth century. It was considered scandalous, and the process was so costly, involving both the Church Courts and a special Act of Parliament, that only the very wealthy could contemplate it. Apparently even the wealthy Rochester (JE) did not consider divorcing his mad wife, and although Helen Huntingdon (TWH) and Mrs Edward Crimsworth (P) leave their husbands, there is no thought of divorce.

Schools, teachers, and governesses

When the first of the Brontë children, Maria and Elizabeth, were old enough to go to school, in 1824, the first rudimentary system of education for all was still ten years away. Boys could attend the public schools, such as Winchester and Eton, if their fathers were wealthy enough; or they could be sent to the private academies, or the local grammar or church school. But schooling for girls was either private, or organised by a charity, or by the church. Most girls did not attend school at all, and many did not have governesses either. As Agnes Grey found, their education consisted of being made 'superficially attractive and showily accomplished' in order to make a satisfactory marriage. Patrick Brontë, however, had other ideas for his daughters.

All the Brontë girls, except Anne, briefly attended the Clergy Daughters' School at Cowan Bridge in Lancashire. The school appears in *Jane Eyre*, with little disguise, as the terrible Lowood, and its manager as the terrifying Mr Brocklehurst. Cowan Bridge was bitterly cold and damp, the food was inadequate, and the girls were harshly treated. The Brontës arrived at various times during 1824, but an outbreak of 'fever' the next year caused the children to be taken home, where Maria and Elizabeth were the first of the family to die of tuberculosis. Whether they contracted it at the school cannot be known, but the dire conditions there must have encouraged it. Charlotte later ascribed her small stature to the inadequacy of the food there; no doubt it was dreadful, but all the Brontës were small, and Charlotte was there for less than a year.

The children spent the next six years at home, reading, writing, and taking lessons with their father. Then in 1831 Charlotte was sent to Miss Wooler's school at Roe Head, a place as different from Cowan Bridge as the tremulous Charlotte could have wished. She achieved such success that three years after she left she was asked to return as a teacher. Emily attended briefly and miserably as a pupil, and was soon replaced by Anne, who stayed for two years. Charlotte did not enjoy her period as a teacher, and resigned in 1838; although there were individual pupils she liked, she thought most of her pupils 'oafs'. Jane Eyre and Lucy Snowe (V) both record the same impression. Meanwhile Emily took up a teaching post at Law Hill in 1837, but seems to have stayed less than a year. These experiences were unpleasant but valuable to both Charlotte and Emily; their knowledge of schools, together with their later experience of the school in Brussels, must have contributed much to the plan they conceived in 1844 of setting up their own school in the parsonage at Haworth.

Meanwhile Charlotte and Anne felt they must contribute to their own support, and to Branwell's, by taking posts as governesses. They both took up appointments with families in Yorkshire, and for the first time experienced the deprivations and humiliations of such a position. Governesses were despised by both their employers and their charges, and they occupied a lonely position between the familiarity of the kitchen and the social grandeur of the drawing-room. Blanche Ingram and her family (JE) speak cruelly in Jane's hearing of her stupidity, and Mrs Pryor (Sh) gives a bitter account of the degradation of a governess's life. Agnes Grey is contemptuously treated, and has to watch helplessly while the crude excesses of the children in her charge are encouraged by their parents. Charlotte and Anne both point to the great difference in treatment between boys and girls at home; while girls are protected as frail and giddy creatures, boys are encouraged to run wild and drink and swear.

The time they spent as governesses left Charlotte and Anne embittered towards the leisured, wealthy classes. As children of the parsonage, they despised the emphasis on material wealth, marriage, 'accomplishments', and superior social airs. Charlotte, especially, came to associate class with discrimination against women. Although no militant feminist, she felt keenly the lack of opportunity offered to women. The genteel occupations such as fine embroidery and lacework she found 'sight-destroying', and a foolish waste of time.

All these experiences, unhappy though most of them were, led the three girls to feel they could manage their own school. But unfortunately their circular on 'The Misses Brontës' Establishment for the Board and Education of a Limited Number of Young Ladies', which was despatched to an uninterested world in 1845, contains only a bare minimum of information. Only Anne seems to have been deeply disappointed when there was no response at all. But it is fortunate that there was none, for they had all by then begun to plan and write their mature work.

Unpublished writings

The four surviving Brontës all began writing before they were ten, and the sagas they started in their childhood continued far into their adult lives. It does not therefore seem appropriate to call this vast amount of writing 'juvenilia'. All the children were astonishingly precocious, and wrote with fluency and zest. Nor was much of this writing mere childish scribbling. Much of it leads directly to their later published work, and often foreshadows their mature writing. In later life Charlotte recognised how much she owed to her youthful writing, and in Emily's work in particular the continuity in growth between Gondal, the poems, and *Wuthering Heights* is plain. Their apprenticeship to writing was in fact completed in early youth, so they were able to produce novels of full maturity when none of them was more than thirty years old.

A vast amount of this early work still exists, equalling in length the published poems and novels. There was also a great deal more, now lost. The entire prose part of Emily's and Anne's huge tale of Gondal has disappeared. No doubt these children would have written anyway, but they seem to have received two early stimulants, one in the form of *Blackwood's Magazine*, and the other in Branwell's box of soliders, given him by his father in 1826. *Blackwood's* opened the world of public events and of all the arts to them. When Charlotte was thirteen, and Branwell a year younger, they produced their own imitation of the magazine, running to fifteen numbers, in tiny script, in tiny bound volumes of about 5.0 x 6.5 cm. These little books set the format for all the Glass Town, Angrian and Gondal stories. There are more than one hundred of them in existence, all written in microscopic print, with sometimes over a thousand words on a page. They were written so small for reasons of economy (paper was expensive), and in order that they might be read by Branwell's soldiers, or 'Young Men'. These soldiers were given names, such as Napoleon and the Duke of Wellington, and their kingdom was established on the coast of Guinea, with Great Glass Town as its capital. Each of the Brontë children, even the youthful Emily and Anne, was granted one of the four Glass Town states, and they all became absorbed in the ever-ramifying stories of the Glass Town Confederacy. For five years, amid much other writing, they created a complex society, involving kings, politics and parliaments, military leaders and armies, as well as poets and artists. Exuberantly, with many dashes and exclamation marks, the children wrote on, ever expanding the adventures, conquests, amours, betrayals and tragedies of the glittering aristocrats of Glass Town. Charlotte's Marquis of Douro (based on the Duke of Wellington's oldest son) eventually conquered the state of Angria, and became the magnificent Duke of Zamorna and eventually the King of Angria ('All here is

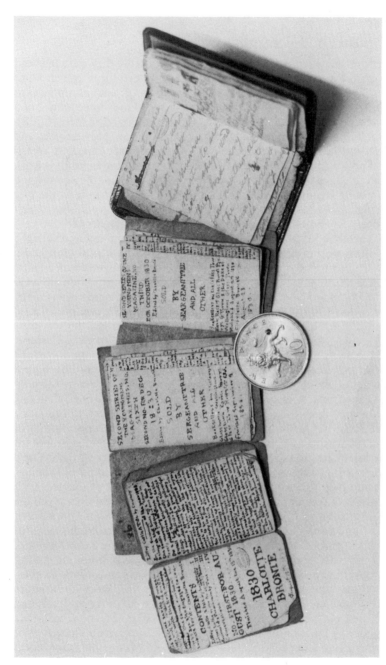

PLATE 2: Some of the tiny books written by Charlotte and Branwell as children.

passion and fire unquenchable'). When Charlotte went to Roe Head in 1835 she contributed less, but the work flowed on from Branwell's prolific pen.

Charlotte's more adult Angrian stories are sharp in observation and character, although still (as she began to realise) much under the influence of Byron. Some, such as the tales of Julia and of Mina Laury, show an advance towards a more realistic outlook. Some of her passages are teasingly humorous at the expense of Branwell but in her later story, 'Captain Henry Hastings', written in 1838–9, her chilling fears for him are already clear. The background of the story is thoroughly Yorkshire, and the heroine Elizabeth, in her longing for love and for a home, is the precursor of Jane (JE), Caroline (Sh), and Lucy (V). In the Angrian tale of Caroline Vernon, probably written in 1839, Charlotte shows a further growth towards a realistic and objective outlook. By then, she had moments when she tired of Angria. Life, she now realised, was not the same as Romance. In a passage often referred to as the 'Farewell to Angria' she wrote, 'I long to quit for a while that burning clime where we have sojourned too long' and intended to 'turn now to a cooler region where the dawn breaks grey and sober'. But the break was not easy, or conclusive; when she was lonely in Brussels in 1843 she found herself still haunted by her imaginary land.

The dominant themes in the Angrian epic are power and love. Power is sought, won and lost; love is the grand passion, driving, ennobling, degrading men and women alike. But there is little development of character, and little in the way of internal conflict. Angrian people may be impassioned, but they are nonetheless static and predictable. In her mature writing Charlotte was to change all this. The major characters of her novels all grow and develop in response to challenge and experience. And in them she was also to challenge the Angrian pattern of male dominance and female submission. Somewhere and somehow, she came to believe, a woman of independent spirit must find a relationship in which she is not crushed.

Long before they had experienced it, the Brontë sisters seem to have understood the force of sexual passion, and to have understood, too, that it does not endure. The amours of the chief characters in both Angria and Gondal endlessly repeat themselves; when Zamorna marries he enjoys 'bliss too perfect to endure'.

After they had disassociated themselves from the Glass Town stories in 1831, Emily and Anne began another saga based on the imaginary island of Gondal. Poems, which have survived, were included in the narrative, often as linkages, and, from a list of names entered by Anne in a school geography book, it is possible to build up some idea of the story. Again the story was of conquest, cruelties, high passions, and battles. The principal monarch was Julius of Almedore, but the dominating character was Augusta Almeda, a creature of wild passion, crimes and caprices, who was, surprisingly, originally based on the young Princess Victoria, later Queen of England. Foreshadowings of *Wuthering Heights* are visible in Augusta, in the tempestuous Julius, and in the weak de Samara. Together out on the moors, Emily and Anne would enact the events and scenes of Gondal, but Anne grew away from it earlier than Emily. As late as 1845 they were playing Gondal rôles together, but by then Anne was no longer whole-heartedly involved.

Emily eventually divided her poems into two notebooks, one set of 'philosophical' poems, and one of the poems of Gondal (see her 'The Poems', pp.117−21). Their abiding themes, which link them closely to *Wuthering Heights*, are found in the world of nature, and in the escape of the soul from mortality.

PLATE 3: Charlotte, *c.* 1839, by J.H. Thompson, a friend of Branwell.

Part 2

Charlotte Brontë

Her life (1816–1855)

Charlotte was born in 1816 at Thornton in North Yorkshire, but when she was four her father became rector of Haworth, near Keighley, and the family moved into the parsonage which was to be Charlotte's home all her life. The year after their arrival her mother died of cancer, and Charlotte never clearly remembered her. Aunt Branwell, who had come to nurse her sister, remained with the household for the rest of her life. Years after, in 1850, her father gave Charlotte her mother's letters to read, and she was greatly moved. Most of her own heroines are motherless, and the affectionate scenes between Caroline and her newly discovered mother in *Shirley* no doubt reveal something of Charlotte's own feelings. It seems likely that the rootless past of these heroines, and their anxious search for secure love, emergé from their author's motherless background.

In 1824 Charlotte was sent to join her two older sisters, Maria and Elizabeth, at the Clergy Daughters' School at Cowan Bridge. The school seemed to Mr Brontë to have good credentials, but it was a harsh, cold place. The chilling damp, the sparseness of the food, and the severity of the teachers and the overseer, are all described in Jane Eyre's account of Lowood. Many of the pupils were ill during the year, and Mr Brontë brought all the girls home again. Maria and Elizabeth both died shortly afterwards from tuberculosis, either contracted at the school or made worse there. The four remaining children received a wide, if unusual, education from their father, and in their free time they began to make up the plays which developed into the sagas of Glass Town, Angria, and Gondal (see 'Home and family' and 'Unpublished writings', pp.11–13 and 23–6 above). Interspersed with her more serious reading, Charlotte secretly enjoyed her aunt's copies of the *Ladies' Magazine*, but her father thought she was wasting time and he burned them.

When Charlotte was fourteen she was sent to school at Roe Head, where at first she was painfully shy; her short-sightedness made her look vague, and her Irish accent was scornfully noted. But she supplemented her eccentric home education with modern languages, enjoyed her food, was brilliantly successful at her work, and made three life-long friends in Ellen Nussey, Mary Taylor, and her headmistress, Miss

Wooler. Much of what we know of Charlotte's views on all manner of topics come from her letters to Ellen Nussey, who preserved their long correspondence.

At home again in 1832, Charlotte helped with the teaching of Emily and Anne, collaborated with Branwell on their huge Angrian romance, drew skilfully, and read voraciously. In 1835 she was offered a teaching post at Roe Head, with a free place as a pupil for Emily. She accepted with some reluctance, but felt she must contribute to the family income, especially as Branwell was expected to become an art student in London. She found herself overworked, lonely, and incapable of liking her pupils. Often haunted by thoughts of Angria and home, she became deeply unhappy, and could not even raise much sympathy for Anne in the religious crisis she was suffering.

In 1836 she sent some of her poems to the poet Robert Southey (1774–1843), but although he was kind he was not encouraging. Acutely depressed, Charlotte left the school on medical advice in 1838, refused a proposal of marriage from Ellen Nussey's brother, and another from a curate, in 1839, and in the same year took up an appointment as governess with the Sidgwick family at Stonegappe. Here again she found herself lonely and unhappy, unsupported in her attempts to teach the rowdy children, and treated as a social inferior by the family. This was her first experience of an occupation which was to appear frequently as a theme in her novels—Jane Eyre, Mrs Pryor (Sh), Lucy Snowe (V), and Frances Crimsworth (P) are all governesses or teachers at some time. While she was at Stonegappe Charlotte visited a house where a madwoman had once been confined in an attic, which may well have suggested Mrs Rochester's confinement in *Jane Eyre*. After a few months, Charlotte left the Sidgwicks with relief.

1840 was a happy year at Haworth. Mr Brontë's new curate, William Weightman (whom Charlotte named 'Celia Amelia'), brought much liveliness into their lives. In 1841 Charlotte took up another post as governess with the White family, near Bradford. Here she was happier, but she disliked leaving home and it was probably about this time that the three sisters began to plan a school of their own at the parsonage. But they were uncertain of their skill in languages, and Charlotte and Emily gratefully accepted their aunt's financial aid to enable them to attend a school in Brussels to improve their French and German. They left early in 1842 and attended a well-organised school, run by a Mme Heger, with some lessons provided by her husband. The sisters worked hard, and greatly improved their linguistic skills, but, hearing of the death of their aunt, returned to Haworth at the end of the year. After a month at home Charlotte returned to Brussels. She was now to spend some hours each week teaching English to M. Heger, and at some time during the two years she was in Brussels she fell painfully in love with him. He was troubled, kind, but apparently unmoved; he is portrayed, in part, in Paul Emanuel in *Villette*. Charlotte had few friends during her second year in Brussels, and became deeply despondent. At the beginning of 1844 she returned home, describing herself as 'tamed and broken'.

The three sisters now devised and published their prospectus for a school, but there was no response, and probably only Anne was greatly disappointed. The feckless Branwell was drinking heavily, and was dismissed from his tutor's post at Thorp Green Hall, causing Charlotte much anguish and exasperation. She continued to write to M. Heger, but was shocked at his suggestion that she should write to him at another address, and ceased to correspond.

It seems she hoped to find some occupation in Paris, and for the first time began to find home life frustrating and irksome. Then in 1845 she came upon some copies of Emily's poems. She was astonished by them, braved Emily's anger, and, after much persuasion, obtained permission to include them, with some of her own and some of Anne's, in a collection for publication. Emily insisted on anonymity, and they called themselves by the deliberately ambiguous names of Currer (Charlotte), Ellis (Emily), and Acton (Anne) Bell. The collection appeared in 1846, and although only two copies were sold, Emily's work received some respectful attention.

Meanwhile the sisters had begun to write their first adult novels, and in 1846 *The Professor*, by Charlotte, *Wuthering Heights*, by Emily, and *Agnes Grey*, by Anne, were sent off to the first of the many publishers who were to reject them. Eventually Emily's and Anne's books were accepted by T.C. Newby, but *The Professor* was rejected (and was not published until after Charlotte's death). Charlotte was deeply dejected, but again set to work, and in the summer of 1847 sent *Jane Eyre* to Smith, Elder and Co. It was accepted enthusiastically, and published in the autumn under the name of Currer Bell. It received excited and widespread attention, ranging from indignant abuse to the high praise of the novelist William Thackeray (1811–63), whom Charlotte greatly admired. *Wuthering Heights* and *Agnes Grey* were then published in the wake of *Jane Eyre*, also under the names of the 'Bells'. In order to sort out their publishers' confusions over their names, Charlotte and Anne set off by train for London, and George Smith (of Smith, Elder and Co.) was astonished to encounter the two 'quaintly dressed little ladies'.

The next two years were terrible ones for Charlotte. By 1848 drink, drugs, and possibly tuberculosis finally overcame Branwell, and he died in September, only three months before Emily's death, also of tuberculosis. Early in the next year it became clear that Anne, too, was affected, and she died in the spring.

While she was nursing her family Charlotte was intermittently writing *Shirley*, which appeared (again under 'Currer Bell''s name) in the autumn of 1849. But her pseudonym no longer protected her, and she embarked on the life of a literary celebrity. George Smith invited her to London, where she saw the sights, admired the paintings of J.M.W. Turner (1775–1851), met the writer Harriet Martineau, and her literary hero, Thackeray. But she was not at ease in fashionable assemblies, and dreaded being presented as a celebrity. Nevertheless, she returned to London again in 1850, when she saw her childhood hero, the Duke of Wellington, met the admiring critic G.H. Lewes (1817–78), and was sketched by the artist George Robinson. Later she toured Scotland with George Smith and his sister, was greatly moved to be in the land of Sir Walter Scott (1771–1832), and found Edinburgh infinitely superior to London. For the first time she met Mrs Gaskell, and stayed with Harriet Martineau in the Lake District. Mrs Gaskell (who was later to write Charlotte's biography) found 'simplicity and power' in her shy guest, and could hardly bring herself to believe that such genius could emerge from so remote a parsonage in the wilds of Yorkshire. In the same year Charlotte wrote a Preface and Memoir for a second edition of *Agnes Grey* and *Wuthering Heights*, and revised some of Emily's work, both the novel and the poems.

In 1851 she again visited London, including the Great Exhibition and the theatre among her expeditions. She began *Villette*, and endured a long period of depression when she was worried about her own and her father's health. At the end of 1852, to her astonishment, she received a proposal of marriage from her father's curate, Arthur Nicholls. Her own uncertainty, and her father's angry opposition, made her postpone her decision, and she left for London just before the publication of *Villette* in January 1853. On this visit she insisted on seeing what she regarded as 'real' things, such as hospitals and prisons. Mr Nicholls left Haworth, but they kept in touch, and by 1854 her father had given up opposing the marriage. Mr Nicholls returned as curate and they were married in June and spent their honeymoon in his native Ireland. In 1855 Charlotte began another novel, to be called *Emma*, but unfortunately her husband did not encourage her. They appear to have been very happy, and when she became ill early in 1855, in the first months of pregnancy, she could not believe she would die. But die she did, at the age of thirty-eight, the last survivor of the six Brontë children. In June her father asked Mrs Gaskell to write a life of his daughter, and in 1857 she published her remarkable 'Life of Charlotte Brontë'.

Writings

Charlotte began writing as a child (see 'Unpublished writings' pp.23–6), and she was still writing in the year of her death. Her known work spans twenty-six years, from her imitations of *Blackwood's Magazine* to her unfinished last novel, *Emma*. She usually wrote rapidly, feeling herself impelled to dash on. Sometimes she was overwhelmed by the need to write; at Roe Head in 1835 she noted, 'I am just going to write because I cannot help it'. She welcomed this creative force, describing it (in the Preface to the 1850 edition of the novels) as 'something that, at times, strangely wills and works for itself'. And she remarks in *Shirley* that 'those who possess this imagination would not give it for gold'. For most of her writing life she did nothing to discourage this urge, which often led her to disregard the stricter requirements of organisation and plot, and made her obstinate about revision. None of her plots achieve the coherence of Emily's or Anne's. She is often tempted to include long irrelevant passages (such as Lucy's visit to London in *Villette*), and she sometimes relies too heavily—especially in *Jane Eyre* and *Villette*—on improbable coincidence. The plot of *Shirley* is astonishingly wayward for a writer of such skill. However, she learned from this novel, and as she became more distrustful of her 'inspiration' she spent more time on her plots. *Villette* is much more solidly constructed, and there are signs that in her last fragment, *Emma*, she intended to discipline her creative urges yet further.

The critic G.H. Lewes, writing on *Villette*, remarked on 'the independent originality of a strong mind nurtured in solitude', and considered that this mind had produced 'a work of astonishing power and passion'. Whatever damage it may have done to her plots, Charlotte's creative drive is responsible for that 'power and passion'. When she is writing at her best, as in the early chapters of *Jane Eyre* or the last scenes of *Villette*, her imagination fuses image and emotion in words which precisely express her intent. The 'strong mind' commented on by Lewes is linked not only with her obvious intelligence, but with the force of her personality. Many narrators like to obliterate themselves, but Charlotte, with her narrow, concentrated vision, always makes her presence felt. So much so that her reader may be allowed to break the prohibition on assuming that writers must be writing of their own experience. Charlotte is almost always writing of her own experience. When she had to write outside it (something she disliked doing, but sometimes had to face), she would set herself to think intently on the event for many nights before she slept, until she believed she understood exactly the experiences she wished to convey.

The limitations of her own experience greatly concerned her as a writer. She felt that novelists who lived more in the world than she did had an advantage. As she bitterly realised, her own experience of the world was limited to that of the motherless daughter of a remote parsonage, of a teacher and a governess, of two years in a school in Brussels, and of falling, once, painfully in love.

In a letter to her publishers written in 1848 she described her belief that a writer's first duty was to follow Truth and Nature, and only then to consider Art. She was determined not to reproduce 'the standard heroes and heroines of novels', but to make characters recognisable beings, even if that meant making them plain and poor. When scenes from her work were criticised, she would retort that at least they were *real*. For the same reason she would not exclude irrelevancy, as long as what it described was true. Falsity she hated above all things.

Love, marriage, isolation, the position of women, and the master/ pupil relationship provide the recurring themes of her work (for the first four of these interests, which are common to all three sisters, see 'Love and marriage', pp.17−21). An abiding interest in the master/ pupil relationship was peculiar to Charlotte, and it was clearly of great significance to her. Three of her heroines are first the pupils, and then the wives (or prospective wives) of their teachers; Frances (P) marries William Crimsworth, Shirley (Sh) marries Louis Moore, and Lucy (V) becomes engaged to M. Paul. Robert Moore (Sh) takes a schoolmasterly interest in Caroline's progress, and Jane Eyre refers to Rochester as 'my master'. Troubled and fascinated as she was by the problems of marriage, Charlotte seems to have seen in the master/pupil relationship a chance of a certain autonomy for the wife. Frances keeps on her school after marriage, and Lucy would perhaps have done the same. And yet, in spite of the spirited views on equality of Frances, Jane, Shirley and Lucy, Charlotte seems to have found some attraction in submission. All the heroines, except perhaps Frances, submit in some degree; even the commanding Shirley seeks a master who will 'curb' her, and both Jane Eyre and Lucy Snowe relish something in the dominant temperaments of their men. This theme of male dominance and female submission is very marked in the Angrian stories, but in her adult work Charlotte often seems to challenge it; yet the suspicion lingers that something in her hankered after domination.

Gothic tales of the supernatural and the macabre reached the height of their fashion about the end of the eighteenth century, in the novels of Horace Walpole (1717−97) and Mrs Radcliffe (1764−1823). Although she did not hold these novels in high esteem, Charlotte employed many of their devices in her Angrian tales, and then returned to them when *The Professor* failed to find a publisher. Her use of dreams and psychic events in *Jane Eyre*, the Banshee wailings and the spectral nun in *Villette*, and her use of preposterous coincidence in both, are among devices which derive from the Gothic, and which made the critic G.H. Lewes warn her against melodrama. She is, however, well aware of the use she is making of this inheritance, and she frequently undermines it with some humorous or explanatory comment which softens an over-dramatic impact; the 'preternatural ... laugh' heard by Jane (JE) occurs at high noon, with 'no circumstance of ghostliness', and the drama of Bertha Rochester's attempt to fire her husband's bed is intentionally undermined by Jane's 'baptising' him with water and hearing his 'anathemas at finding himself in a pool'. In *Shirley*, as in *The Professor*, Charlotte deliberately did without these devices, but in *Villette* she again made her own highly conscious use of what they had to offer. Writing at her best, Charlotte can use these Gothic contrivances to powerful symbolic effect, as in Lucy's (V) disposal of the empty trappings of the 'nun', and in her eventual understanding of the bizarre masque in the Park as 'timber, paint and pasteboard'.

Charlotte was also deeply influenced by the Romantic poet Byron (1788–1824) and the novelist Sir Walter Scott. As a child she was fascinated by both (see 'Unpublished writings', pp.23–6), and she continued to write verse and stories in a high Romantic vein until her twenty-fourth year, when she bade her 'farewell to Angria'. Even then, Byronic heroics did not entirely lose their attraction, and her thoughts were often on Angria when she was on her own in Brussels in 1843. And when she realised that the plain, realistic manner of *The Professor* was not going to find her a publisher, she returned to the familiar model of the Byronic hero and put something of him into Rochester. The master of Thornfield is at first sight not handsome, but with his flashing eyes, his darkness, his mystery, and his passionate past, he is as Byronic as the heroes of Angria.

Charlotte's deep admiration for the poems and novels of Scott led her to write to her friend Ellen Nussey in 1834 that 'all novels after his are worthless' (although when she discovered Thackeray's work she changed her mind on this). She enjoyed the sensational element in Scott's work; the death of Mrs Rochester, in the fire she had herself started, has a possible source in the death of Ulrica in *Ivanhoe* (1819). Nevertheless, when it was required of her, as in her historical work *Shirley*, Charlotte was able to cast off Scott's influence, and portray recent, recognisable social history stripped of fantasy and romance.

The problem of a woman's place in society—what we would now call 'the position of women'—was close to Charlotte's heart. Although no militant feminist, she felt that girls should be educated, and allowed to prepare themselves to earn their own living if necessary. Writing to Mr Williams, her publisher's reader, in 1848, Charlotte looked forward to the day when there would be a place for 'female lawyers, female doctors, female engravers' and more writers and artists. She wished that every woman in England might have the opportunity of education and a career. All her heroines are women who work, Shirley (Sh) at her estate, Frances (P), Jane (JE), and Lucy (V) at their teaching. And Caroline (Sh) does her best to persuade her intransigent uncle to allow her to become a governess. Charlotte abhorred the usual custom by which a young woman did nothing but wait about for marriage. She was equally perturbed by the fate of the unmarried woman, the 'spinster' or 'old maid'. Following the heartless custom of the time, William Crimsworth (P) described spinsters as 'fashioned out of a little parchment and much bone'. Charlotte told Mr Williams that she considered the lives of those who remained at home unmarried were worse than those of servants, and their disappointment would inevitably 'degrade their nature'. In defence of spinsters she created some touching portraits, such as those of Miss Ainley and Miss Mann (Sh). Although they are poor, ignored, and deprived of affection, they live with dignity and spirit. In 1846 Charlotte told her old headmistress, Miss Wooler, that there was no more respectable a character than an unmarried woman 'who makes her own way through life quietly, perseveringly'.

Charlotte's experience as a governess left her embittered about the wealthy, leisured classes. It was not until late in her life that she encountered wealth combined with kindness. With the exception of Rochester and Shirley, all her chief characters, and all whom she admires, are people who have to earn their own living. The wealthy, such as the Ingrams (JE) or the Sympsons (Sh), do not command her respect, and indeed some are overdrawn to the point of caricature. However, she had no illusions about poverty either. She saw it all about her in rural Yorkshire, and it seems likely that Robert Moore (Sh) is speaking for her when he describes poverty as 'selfish, contracted, grovelling, anxious'. Charlotte's sympathy with the lives of the poor is particularly evident in *Shirley* in the poverty of William Farren, in the kindness of Mr Hall, and in Robert's change from indifference to an understanding of their plight.

Indeed Charlotte's sympathy is always most strongly moved, and her imagination most deeply stirred, by the unhappy, the lonely, and the unfortunate. Those who must toil up John Bunyan's (1628–88) Hill of Difficulty in his *Pilgrim's Progress*, like Jane (JE), Caroline (Sh) and Lucy (V), are those who engross her attention. The people on whom fortune smiles, such as Dr Bretton and Paulina (V), do not capture her interest to the same degree. Among the minor characters it is the crippled Harry Sympson (Sh), the spinsters Ainley and Mann (Sh), and the invalid Miss Marchmont (V) who evoke the most memorable portraits. By the time she wrote *Villette* Charlotte had come to believe that certain lives were blessed, while 'Other lives run from the first another course'. The contrast between the easy happiness of the

Brettons and the long anguish of Lucy (V) is always evident. But it is not observed with rancour; the blessed may also be the beautiful and good, like Graham and Paulina (V)—'Nature's elect, harmonious and benign'.

The injustices of life never shook Charlotte's faith in the ultimate mercy of God. There is no hint in novels or letters that the suffering she experienced, and saw all about her, challenged this faith. She deeply distrusted and disliked the atheism of her friend, Harriet Martineau.

Although in a time of despair in Brussels in 1843 Charlotte made a Catholic confession, she heartily disliked the Roman Catholic Church, and felt no more sympathy for Methodism, which in *Shirley* she identifies with anarchy (see 'Religion and the Church' pp.15–17). Like her father, she took her stand with those in the Church of England who put their emphasis on good works, simple godly living, and the mercy of God. Like him, she despised the elaborate ritual of the high Church and the Puseyites (see 'Religion and the Church'). Love, religion, and the effects of wealth, are among her most constant themes, and in several of her plots they are closely related. Each, she feels, may provide a tangle of problems, but where love is strong even the most painful difficulties will be solved; Paul Emanuel and Lucy (V) do not permit even their different religions to stand between them, Shirley and Louis (Sh) are in the end not daunted by the discrepancy in their wealth and status.

Charlotte was in fact sharply aware of the major issues of her time, especially those with a religious or social bent. But she was also open to more ephemeral excitements. The theory of phrenology, which held that the 'bumps' on the skull contained 'organs' responsible for character, explains some phrases which seem baffling today. Jane (JE) noted that Rochester's forehead showed 'a solid enough mass of intellectual organs', and he in his turn found Jane's love of Thornfield arose from her 'organ of Adhesiveness'. Another popular theory found the clue to character not in the skull but in the form and expression of the face; on various occasions, as when M. Paul first looks over Lucy (V), character is confidently predicted from the face.

Charlotte is frequently accused of having little sense of humour. It is true that her attempts at humour are sometimes cumbersome; the 'comic' curates in *Shirley*, and Shirley's own attempts at sprightly conversation, are distinctly leaden. Yet to say she has no humour is unjust. In *Shirley* in particular there are some descriptive passages worthy of Jane Austen (1775–1817); Hortense Moore, for example, in her capacity as Robert's housekeeper, always wears a vast apron because 'she appeared to think that by means of it she somehow effected a large saving in her brother's income'. Of Miss Mann Charlotte writes that 'to avoid excitement was one of Miss Mann's aims in life: she had been composing herself ever since she came down in the morning, and had just attained a certain lethargic state of tranquillity when the visitor's knock at the door startled her, and undid her day's work'. And the descriptions of the ladies of the Sympson family are dryly, masterfully ironic; the girls are 'chilled with decorous dread' in the presence of the lively Shirley, and at all times 'nothing could exceed the propriety of their behaviour'. Although Charlotte can occasionally sustain scenes of high comedy, such as that in which Malone (Sh) comes courting Caroline in the drawing-room, it is in sharp, brief comment that her humour excels.

Some of her characters, such as Yorke Hunsden (P), Malone (Sh), and the explosive little M. Paul (V), are clearly intended to raise a smile. The fact that the effort is often unconvincing has less to do with Charlotte's humour than with her difficulty in creating and presenting character. In this particular aspect of her writing she does not seem to have trusted that inventiveness which carried her surging through a narrative. And she felt at a disadvantage in trying to portray a wider range of people than the narrow circle she knew. This distrust of her own powers seems to have led to the use of real people as models, as if her imagination required some real, remembered object to impel it. While Rochester and perhaps M. Paul owe much to her imagination, Shirley, Caroline and the Yorkes (Sh), Graham Bretton and Mme Beck (V), Helen Burns, Miss Temple (JE), and many others throughout the novels, are solidly based on people Charlotte knew. The longest and most complex portrait of a known person is that of Shirley, intended (as Mrs Gaskell informs us) to be Emily as she might have been 'had she been placed in health and prosperity'. But even when using models Charlotte's characters sometimes lose definition, and become yet again the mouthpieces of their creator. Her own personality is so strong that Charlotte can easily lose the focus of her character and reveal herself instead. In the novels in which she is herself the narrator (JE, V), one would expect the characterisation of the heroine to be stronger, and indeed this is so.

Charlotte's chief female model was of course herself. Jane Eyre and Lucy Snowe (V) are in many respects barely concealed self-portraits. Their experiences of home, of genteel poverty, of teaching as schoolmistresses and governesses, directly reflect Charlotte's own life; and in their physical plainness, their intellectual powers, and their social inadequacy, they reflect Charlotte's feelings about herself.

With her male characters Charlotte had particular difficulty. For the first two-thirds of her life she knew very few men, other than Branwell, her father, and his curates. With the exception of M. Paul (V), her attempts at building male characters tend to be over-analytic, as with Bretton (V) and St John Rivers (JE), resulting in a stiff catalogue of qualities; or, like Rochester, conceived in a flight of Byronic fancy, from which emerged the kind of dark, virile, unmannerly maleness which so fascinated all the Brontë sisters.

In spite of these limitations, however, most of Charlotte's characters exhibit strength of feeling which means they are never dull or dead. Whatever their inconsistencies, they suffer, rage, weep, and love intensely. And what is more, the best of them grow. Frances (P), Jane (JE), Caroline (Sh) and Lucy (V) are none of them the same women at the end of their stories as they were at the beginning. All suffer greatly, and through their suffering they become stronger, fuller, and wiser. Courage was a quality Charlotte greatly admired. Physical bravery is shown by several of her characters, especially by Moore (Sh) facing the rioters, by Rochester (JE) at the burning of Thornfield, and by Shirley's cauterising of her own arm with a red-hot iron. But the courage of dogged perseverance, through isolation and pain, is a courage Charlotte admired even more; Lucy (V) reflects often upon the necessity of this kind of private, daily strength, and it is shown in some form by all Charlotte's heroines.

She was not interested in paragons of virtue, any more than in monsters of vice. Her passion for 'Truth and Nature', and her scorn for the idealised heroes and heroines of popular fiction, led her to create characters who were far from faultless. In *Shirley* she boldly assures the reader that 'every character in this book will be found to be more or less imperfect, my pen refusing to draw anything in the model line'. Her other books are equally peopled with deeply flawed characters; Rochester (JE) and Robert Moore (Sh) both behave with selfish cruelty, M. Paul (V) is a petty tyrant, and Lucy (V) finds herself 'jealous and haughty' and 'full of faults'. Only two of the heroines (Shirley and Caroline) are pretty, and none of the men are handsome; Rochester (JE) and M. Paul (V) are positively plain, and the Moores (Sh) are both bony, sallow men. Grecian good looks are always associated with men who are treacherous, like de Hamal (V), or cold, like Rivers (JE).

Charlotte's prose is remarkably varied. In one paragraph (as in *Shirley*, Chapter 2) it can rise from short, staccato sentences to a long, graceful line. At its best, as in the early chapters of *Jane Eyre*, it varies in precise accord with whatever the author wishes to express. Swift, certain in tone, and very markedly Charlotte's own, it is vigorous more often than it is smooth, and often filled with striking imagery. But it can also be awkwardly contorted, and sometimes choked with over-emphasis or personification. The didactic style, in which she addresses the reader, can be prim and pompous, and her excursions into 'fine writing' (as in Shirley's discourse on Eve) can be unhappily turgid. On the evidence of the unfinished *Emma*, it seems that at the time of her death Charlotte was aiming at a more austere prose style.

Throughout her adult writing, her debt to the Bible is profound, standing above all other influences on her language. Biblical images, phrases, and longer passages, fall naturally, without quotation-marks, into conversation and description, especially in moments of high emotion; Caroline (Sh) passes into 'the valley of the shadow of death', and after her marriage to Rochester Jane (JE) becomes 'bone of his bone and flesh of his flesh'.

Of all the senses, sight dominates the imagery in Charlotte's work. In spite of a few striking images which derive from other senses, such as the dreadful bells at Lowood (JE), and the smell of Rochester's cigar in the garden (JE), these other senses are of small account in comparison with sight. Much of the writing is as full of imagery as a poet's. A particular skill lies in sharp, brief description; Mme Beck's (V) lips are 'like a thread', the Misses Sympson (Sh) 'were tall, with a Roman nose apiece', and Mrs Harden (JE) is 'made up of equal parts of whalebone and iron'. Charlotte always enjoyed appearances, and found them revealing of character.

Like Emily, she turns constantly for her imagery to the world of nature, where she could find forms and symbols powerful enough to embrace the passions she wished to describe. She was not interested in the detail of trees or animals or flowers, but she was strongly drawn to the wide spaces of moorland, vivid sunsets, clouds, moonscapes, and the tumult of wind and sea. These images are used to convey and to intensify emotion, and they are also used to bind her stories together. Fire, frost, and the colour crimson run through *Jane Eyre*; shipwreck, wind and storm bind the beginning and end of *Villette*. Indeed weather is always on Charlotte's mind. Whether it is the fresh spring sun which shines on Shirley and Caroline on their walk (Sh), or 'the dreary fellowship with the winds' experienced by Lucy (V), Charlotte uses it constantly to reinforce mood.

Her liking for personification is yet another aspect of her strongly visual sense. She is more at ease when she can visualise the abstract, and cast it in living form. Innumerable abstractions, such as Conviction, Truth, Recognition, and Falsehood appear scattered throughout her work. Sometimes they succeed in concentrating an idea, but often they add little for the reader of today, and sometimes they distract.

Another favourite practice of Charlotte's, also uncertain in its effect, is her habit of addressing the reader directly. The device is used both to encourage attention, and to create intimacy, and in these aims it may sometimes be successful. But frequently it has less happy effects. Too easily it becomes coy, as in 'I am aware, reader, and you need not remind me . . . ' (Sh), or an excuse for a confused narrative, as in 'I have told you, reader . . . ' (JE). The celebrated 'Reader, I married him' (JE) is probably the most famous line in Charlotte's work.

Charlotte seems to have been happiest writing in the first person. Only one of her novels, *Shirley*, is objectively narrated, and she returned to the first person for *Villette* and the unfinished *Emma*. The method seems to have been well suited to her strong, self-absorbed personality, and her first-person novels have a unity almost entirely absent in *Shirley*, where there is no steady centre. Charlotte's identification with Jane (JE) and Lucy (V) gives their lives an intensity shared by no other characters in the novels. In spite of the limitations of a first-person narrative, both novels remain consistent, and (with the exception of their coincidences) credible. Charlotte's aptitude for this form may be connected with her problems in creating character. The 'I' narrative enables her to identify with her heroines in such a way that she could make direct use of her own feelings and experience.

She was clearly very careful about the names of her chief characters. She changed her original 'Lucy Frost' to 'Lucy Snowe' (V); 'Rochester' (JE) carries hints of the wild passionate poet, the Earl of Rochester (1647–80); 'Eyre' is an old word meaning 'journey', and also carries echoes of 'eyrie' and 'eerie'; 'Moore' (Sh) suggests rock and sturdiness. Nor was she afraid of biblical overtones; 'Emanuel' (V) implies salvation, and St John Rivers (JE) carries overtones of John the Baptist.

The Professor

Summary

William Crimsworth describes, in a letter to an old school-fellow, how he was reluctantly educated by two wealthy uncles. When grown up, he sets off to find his older brother, Edward, a prosperous mill-owner in the North. Edward gives him employment as a clerk, but he is a harsh man, and at his birthday celebrations he ignores William. The young man meets another local businessman, Yorke Hunsden, whom he finds blunt but intriguing. William becomes aware of his brother's dislike of him, and he begins to detest his work. By chance, he is asked into Hunsden's house, and told he will never make a tradesman.

The next day Edward accuses him of blackening his name in the town, and attempts to whip him. William angrily resigns, and when he returns to his lodging he finds Hunsden, who gives him an introduction to a friend in Brussels. Excitedly William arrives in Brussels, and is offered a post as English teacher in a school run by the affable M. Pelet. He manages his slow Flemish pupils well, and is soon offered more teaching at the next-door girls' school, run by the pretty young Mlle Reuter.

He contrives to quell the flirtatious beauties in the front row of his class, and acquits himself well in a searching interview with the clever

Mlle Reuter. His original vision of female innocence and charm is cruelly destroyed by the foolish, deceitful pupils, but Mlle Reuter is charming to him and he begins to think of love. Then one evening he hears her and M. Pelet discussing their marriage plans, and feels he can have no more faith in love. He understands Pelet's guile, and makes plain to Mlle Reuter that he has overheard them.

A young pupil-teacher, Mlle Frances Henri, is recommended to him for English lessons. He finds her an admirable student, but a reluctant teacher. He is amazed by the power and originality of her compositions, but finds her manner shy and mysterious. He takes every opportunity of speaking to her, although Mlle Reuter constantly and jealously interrupts them. He finds she was born in Geneva, of an English mother, and now lives with her aunt in Brussels, where she pays for her education by making lace. She longs to see England, and live again among Protestants.

William remains somewhat aloof, but he gives her encouragement, and is pleased with her growing confidence. Then abruptly she disappears, and the jealous Mlle Reuter informs him that she has left, leaving no address. He is angry and disappointed, but Frances leaves him a grateful note, and some money for her lessons. For a month he trudges Brussels looking for her, then one day finds her weeping in the Protestant cemetery, where her aunt now lies. He realises how greatly he loves her, and is determined to make her his wife. They have tea in her poor lodging, and he finds Mlle Reuter knew her address all the time. When he returns to the school he angrily resigns from his post.

Mlle Reuter has embarrassingly fallen in love with William, and one night M. Pelet returns home drunk and tries to murder him. William now resigns his post at M. Pelet's school as well, and is left jobless, homeless, and almost penniless. Soon he hears that Frances has obtained a job as a teacher, and that Yorke Hunsden is soon to arrive in Brussels. In desperation for employment he visits a school-parent, who owes him a favour, but finds him away from home.

Hunsden's stringent presence both pleases and unsettles him. Hunsden tells him that Edward had been declared bankrupt, and his wife had left him, but he was now again in business. William manages to see the parent, Vandenhuten, who secures him an excellent teaching post in a Brussels school. In great excitement William goes to Frances's lodging, and asks her to marry him. She declares her love and devotion to her 'master', but she is adamant that she will not give up her teaching when they marry.

A year and a half after their simple wedding, they open their own school in Brussels. For ten years they prosper, then return with their son, Victor, to England. There they settle near Yorke Hunsden, and lead a country life of great content.

General commentary

Charlotte's first novel, it was rejected by seven publishers, and was not published until 1857, two years after her death. She described how 'the chill of despair' invaded her when Emily's and Anne's novels were finally accepted, but hers was not. Looking back on *The Professor* in 1847 she found the beginning 'very feeble', but she was pleased with the parts relating to Brussels, and determined to re-cast the story into a full three-volume work, which eventually became *Villette*.

But the novel is of interest in itself, not only as a quarry for *Villette*. Charlotte was probably right in believing that the book was rejected because it was (as she wrote in her Preface) deliberately 'plain and homely', lacking in 'the wild, wonderful, and thrilling', and altogether lacking in an 'ornamented and redundant style'. It is probably the first English novel set largely in a school, and it is sustained by themes and characters which become familiar in Charlotte's later work. She drew upon much of her most intense experience for this novel. Her period in Brussels (1842–4), the school, its teachers, and her own painful experience of love are all used as raw material for the story. Her own relationship with M. Heger is reversed, in that the schoolmaster (William) is English, and the pupil (Frances) is half-French. Although Mlle Reuter and M. Pelet do not appear to be close portraits of the Hegers, they share some of the characteristics which were later more fully developed in Mme Beck and M. Paul Emanuel (V).

Plot, structure and themes

The plot is simple, following directly the course of Crimsworth's life, career, and loves. But the structure of the early part is awkward, as Charlotte recognised. The opening letter to Charles is a clumsy device, and the time William spends in the northern English town lacks the lively interest of his life in Brussels.

As Charlotte describes in her Preface, the themes of her story were to be based on real life, without recourse to flights of romance. Often throughout the book the author, speaking through Crimsworth, comments on the contrast between the worlds of the real and of the romantic. As described in the Preface, the hero was to 'work his way through life' as real men worked, with no assistance from sudden good fortune. As always with Charlotte, the theme of a woman's place in marriage and in society is prominent. William expects that after their marriage Frances will give up her teaching, but she has no intention of doing so, and cannot tolerate the idea that she should be 'kept' by him merely as an ornament to his home. Charlotte's contempt for Mlle Reuter's belief that women should not be writers is expressed with ironic force; and so too is her sympathy for the unmarried, seen by William as beings without hearts, 'fashioned out of a little parchment and much bone'.

The master-pupil relationship is established as a theme which was to reappear in each of Charlotte's novels. William first meets Frances when she is sent to him for English lessons, and it is on this basis that their relationship develops. But eventually she becomes a teacher in her own right, owns her own school, and regards herself as an intellectual equal in their marriage.

Love is presented without romantic raptures. For both William and Frances it is deep and strong, but it is based on the domestic hearth; for Mlle Reuter it is a matter of flirtation, and for M. Pelet an affair of jealousy and violence. Sensuality is more openly expressed than in any of Charlotte's later works. M. Pelet's description of his beautiful pupils, and William's feeling for Mlle Reuter, who made him feel 'barbarous and sensual as a pasha', are expressed with great frankness for the time.

A concern with social justice (which was to reappear strongly in *Shirley*) is vigorously expressed by the radical Hunsden, who detests the contrast between the starving, disease-ridden poor, and the easy, over-fed lives of their masters. Religious faith (another abiding theme of Charlotte's) appears as a minor but significant interest. Frances is presented as a devout Swiss Protestant, who longs to live in Protestant England; and William feels that Mlle Reuter might have been an honest woman, had she been a Protestant.

Narration and style

This is the only one of Charlotte's novels in which the narrator is a man. Her difficulties are made clear in the unfocused character of William, who is convincing neither as a man nor as a narrator. Too often his voice slips into Charlotte's recognisable tones. The narration is earnest and didactic, with high emphasis on moral endeavour. It has the vigour and readability of all Charlotte's writing, including her inventiveness with imagery and verbs, but it lacks the variety of the later books. Many of her favourite devices make their first appearance here—invocations and asides to the Reader, the use of French, and a heavy reliance on personification. Seasons and weather were always of interest to Charlotte, and here they are used, as so often later, to reinforce mood or event; when William at last finds Frances again, a superb sunset spreads across the sky, and later their warm, domestic love is heightened by contrast with the cold and snow without.

Characters

Several of these are preliminary sketches of the characters who people *Villette:*

Frances Henri: Frances is an independent, warm, intelligent girl, who pays for her own lessons by lace-mending. She survives her dismissal, her aunt's death, and the loss of William with courage, before she finds security as a teacher. She has the spirit to stand up to the aggressive Hunsden, and insists that she retains her teaching post after marriage. She has little of Lucy Snowe's repressed emotional fervour, but they have much else in common.

William Crimsworth: William's moral worth is immediately made plain when he refuses his uncle's offer of a living in the Church, and the hand in marriage of a wealthy cousin. Three times he resigns an appointment on principle; once when his brother accuses him, again when he discovers that Mlle Reuter has concealed Frances's address, and the third time when M. Pelet attacks him. At first he is much attracted by the flirtatious and deceitful Mlle Reuter, but he despises her conduct, and his love for Frances grows strongly and surely. With great perseverance he finds her again, and then, by diligence and enterprise, they both obtain an income sufficient for them to return to England, ten years later, with their son.

Yorke Hunsden: A blunt, stringent radical, he is clearly the original of Hiram Yorke in *Shirley*. He is harsh and aggressive, but his heart is kind; he buys the picture of William's mother, advises William on money, and helps to support the school.

Mlle Reuter: She is a charming, confident 'directrice' who runs her school with secret watchfulness, in the manner of Mme Beck in *Villette*. She is charmed by William, but he finds out in time that she is superficial and deceitful. She conceals her relationship with M. Pelet, dismisses Frances when she observes William's growing attachment to her, and pretends she does not know the girl's address. Her character is no doubt partly based on that of Mme Heger (see 'Life', pp.27–31), but Mme Beck (V) is a more fully developed portrait of that lady.

Jane Eyre

Summary

Jane begins her story as a ten-year-old orphan in the house of her aunt, Mrs Reed. The Reed children, Eliza, John and Georgiana, are petted and indulged, while Jane is bullied and rebuffed. When she resists their bullying, she is dragged off by the servants, Abbot and Bessie, and locked up in the 'red room', where she becomes hysterical and loses consciousness. She comes round in her own bed, with the kindly apothecary, Mr Lloyd, standing beside her. He shows some understanding of her unhappiness, and tells Mrs Reed she would be better away at school. Still defiant, Jane is soon faced with Mr Brocklehurst, the Principal of Lowood School. Mrs Reed tells him that Jane is deceitful, and when he is gone Jane gives vent to her outrage. To her amazement, Mrs Reed is frightened and subdued.

Jane arrives at Lowood, where she is greeted kindly by the Superintendent, Miss Temple. But the school is bitterly cold and austere; work is hard and the food inedible. Jane makes friends with the gentle Helen Burns, whose Christian faith enables her to tolerate all injustices. During a history lesson Helen is beaten by the teacher, and Jane, who feels oppression should be fought, is bewildered by Helen's acceptance.

Mr Brocklehurst lectures the girls on the virtues of poverty and plain living; the elaborate toilette of his own wife and daughters emphasises his hypocrisy. Remembering Mrs Reed's accusation, he points out Jane as a liar, and she endures her ordeal only through the sympathy of Helen. Miss Temple asks Jane for her story, and gets in touch with Mr Lloyd, who clears Jane of Mrs Reed's accusation. Jane takes heart, and realises that even Lowood is better than living with the Reeds. When typhus strikes the school many of the girls die, and others go home. Jane realises that Helen is dying of tuberculosis, and late at night creeps into her bed. Helen assures Jane of her calm faith in God, and dies in Jane's arms.

Jane remains at Lowood for another eight years, during which the regime is a little improved. She becomes Head of School, and then a teacher for two years. But when Miss Temple leaves to marry, she finds herself a post as a governess. Just before she leaves, the Reeds' servant, Bessie, arrives to see her, and tells her that her unknown uncle from Madeira had called to ask for her seven years before.

Jane arrives as governess at Thornfield Hall, where she is welcomed by the pleasant housekeeper, Mrs Fairfax. She discovers that the master of the house is Mr Rochester, who is usually away, and that her pupil is his ward, Adèle. A mysterious woman, Grace Poole, lives at the top of the house. Jane is content with Adèle and Mrs Fairfax for company, but feels that women require challenge as much as men.

After some three months, Jane meets a rider on the road, who falls from his horse on the ice. She assists him, and finds on her return that he is her employer, Mr Rochester. He summons Jane and demands to know her history. He finds Adèle is much improved, and is impressed by the power of Jane's painting. Some days later he summons her again, and questions her imperiously on many matters. Jane is polite but firm, refusing to submit tamely to his views. The sympathy between them grows, and after a few weeks Rochester tells her about the mistress he had in Paris. She had assured him Adèle was his, so he had adopted the child. Jane protests that she loves Adèle no less because of this. She perceives Rochester's interest in her, and recognises her own growing feeling for him.

When that night she hears a noise, she rushes from her bed, and sees smoke coming from Rochester's room. His bedding is on fire, and she extinguishes it with water. Agitatedly he tells her it must have been Grace Poole who fired the bed, and he seems on the verge of declaring his love. Jane is surprised when the next day Grace Poole calmly advises her to lock her door at night. When Mrs Fairfax tells Jane that Rochester has gone away to visit the beautiful Blanche Ingram, Jane upbraids herself for her romantic fancies, and dismisses her hopes of love.

Rochester arrives back with a party of guests, and Jane and Adèle are summoned to the drawing-room. The fashionable guests, who include the beautiful Blanche, speak disdainfully about governesses. As she watches her master and Blanche behave flirtatiously together, Jane realises how much she has come to love him. She tries to escape her pain by leaving the room, but Rochester sees her go and follows her, speaking some kind words.

Jane watches Blanche and feels that Rochester does not truly love her, but seeks a conventional, socially acceptable marriage. Her contempt for Blanche is such that she cannot feel jealous, in spite of the depth of her love for Rochester. When he is briefly away, a young man, Richard Mason, arrives from the West Indies to see him. The same evening an old gypsy woman calls, and demands to tell the fortunes of all the party. She tells Jane she should not resist love, and asks what she thinks of her master's courtship of Blanche. Jane's reply is careful, and the old woman tells her that her character will always be open to 'that still small voice which interprets the dictates of conscience'. The gypsy reveals herself as Rochester, and Jane protests at the trick. When she tells him of Mason's arrival he is perturbed, and admits how much he depends on her.

That night the household is aroused by a scream. When Rochester has persuaded his guests to return to bed, he asks Jane to help him upstairs, where Mason has been badly wounded with a knife. Jane assumes his attacker is Grace Poole and is left for two hours attending Mason, while Rochester fetches a doctor. At dawn, when Mason has gone, Rochester asks Jane whether a young man who has committed a wrong in youth has the right to hope for a second chance. Jane replies that these things lie with God.

Jane is summoned to the Reeds, where she finds her aunt very ill. John is dead, Eliza has become a religious fanatic, and Georgiana is worldly and lazy. Mrs Reed confesses that three years before this time Jane's uncle had wished to make her his heir, but she had told him Jane was dead. Jane is forgiving, but Mrs Reed dies still hating her.

Jane returns to Thornfield, where everyone is welcoming. She tells Rochester of her joy in returning, and is puzzled to find no preparations for his marriage to Blanche. Midsummer Eve is warm and sweet, and Rochester surprises Jane out in the garden. When he suggests a post for her in Ireland when he is married, she breaks down and confesses her love. He is greatly moved, and asks her to marry him. After much explanation and bewilderment, Jane joyfully accepts, and they retreat to the house as an ominous thunderstorm breaks.

Jane's happiness does not overwhelm her independence. Although Rochester wishes to shower her with luxuries, she refuses most of them and continues to teach Adèle. Rochester objects to her 'hardness' but admires her spirit. Shortly before the wedding Jane is restless, and she tells Rochester of two painful dreams, which were followed by a visit to her room of an evil-looking woman, who tore her wedding-veil in two, and caused her to faint with terror. Rochester is shaken, and says it must have been Grace Poole.

During the marriage ceremony in the church the next day, one of the strangers present objects, saying that Rochester is already married to Bertha Mason. The other stranger, who turns out to be Richard Mason, states that Bertha is still living at Thornfield. Swearing angrily, Rochester returns to the house and exhibits the mad Bertha. Jane now realises that it was she, and not Grace Poole, who tore her veil. Mason's friend, Briggs, says he has come on behalf of Jane's uncle, who is dying in Madeira. Jane eventually retires to bed, overcome by grief. In great anguish, she decides she must leave Rochester. The next day he begs her to live with him, married or no, and describes how he was tricked into marrying the wealthy Bertha, whose mind soon became unhinged. He had finally established her under Grace's guard at Thornfield, and begun to live on the continent. He tells Jane that he sees her as his only salvation. Although she is deeply moved, she does not weaken, and before dawn next morning creeps away and boards a stage-coach.

For four days, cold, starving, and eventually near death, Jane wanders the moors beyond Whitcross. When she comes upon a small, lonely house she begs to be let in, and she is given a meal and put to bed. Three days later she comes downstairs, and meets the two friendly sisters of the Rivers family, Diana and Mary, and their brother, St John. The young women are governesses on holiday, and their brother is a cleric. Jane tells them a little of her story, and asks help in finding work, as she is homeless and without family. Her new friends insist she stays with them meanwhile.

After a while St John offers Jane the post of village teacher, which she gratefully accepts. A letter arrives for the Rivers family, telling them that their wealthy uncle has left them nothing in his will. Diana and Mary leave to return to their posts. Jane is discouraged by her school, but finds independence preferable to being a mistress indulged in luxury. St John tells her of his determination to become a missionary in India. A beautiful local girl, Rosamond Oliver, tempts him greatly, but he refuses to court her. Jane begins to enjoy her school, but she cannot forget Rochester.

St John has discovered Jane's history, and tells her that she is the heir of her uncle, Mr Eyre of Madeira, who has left her a fortune. Jane is stunned, and extracts from St John the fact that he and his sisters are her cousins. Her delight is unbounded, because now she has relations, and money too. She insists on dividing the fortune equally between the four of them.

Jane closes the school at Christmas, when Diana and Mary return home. But St John becomes overbearing, insisting that she learn Hindustani with him, and in the spring he proposes that she go to India with him as his wife, even though he does not love her. She has now lost all hope of Rochester, and says she will go as his companion, but will not marry him. He is bitterly resentful, and exerts a strange hypnotic pressure on her to accept his proposal. She is on the point of giving in when suddenly, in her mind, she hears a cry from Rochester, calling for her help, and she answers his cry.

The next day she sets out for Thornfield, but when she arrives a day and a half later she finds it a blackened ruin. She discovers that it was burnt down by Bertha, who perished in the fire, while Rochester lost his sight and his left hand. He is now at his other house, Ferndean, thirty miles away. Jane finds him there, blind and helpless. He is at first unbelieving, then overwhelmed with joy. They arrange their marriage, and realise that each heard the despairing cry of the other.

Writing ten years after the event, Jane finds their marriage perfect. Rochester has recovered the sight of one eye, and is able to see their first-born son. The last lines of the book are with St John Rivers, who will soon die in his noble Christian service in India.

The writing of *Jane Eyre*

Charlotte did not begin *Jane Eyre* until she was thirty. *The Professor* had been rejected seven times, and she knew she must try something less sober and more arresting. She began writing in the summer of 1846, and finished a year later. Smith, Elder and Co. were greatly impressed, and accepted the book with alacrity, publishing it in October 1847.

Plot and structure

Charlotte's novels are not notable for conventional plotting and structure, and *Jane Eyre* is no exception. The first quarter of the story concerns Jane as a child; the next half covers her growing relationship with Rochester; and most of the last quarter follows her connection with the Rivers family, reverting to Rochester again only in the last three chapters. The story involves three separate families, and five separate settings; were it not for Jane herself their fragile connections would amount to little more than the fact that Jane's uncle in Madeira is related to both the Reeds and the Riverses. Added to this, the story is full of improbabilities and unlikely coincidences. It is highly improbable that Jane should never seriously consider the mystery of Grace Poole and the attic; and it is incredible that the house she manages to reach when she is half dead of exposure should be that of her cousins.

Yet in spite of these deficiencies, the novel does have an unmistakable unity, and a narrative drive and conviction which reduce the improbabilities to insignificance. The unity derives almost entirely from Jane herself. Her narrative in the first person appears so convincing and genuine an experience that almost alone it binds the work together. The tone of the writing is so delicately judged that Jane can occupy the centre of the entire book without ever becoming tedious, over-obtrusive or over-diffident. She invites the reader to identify with her, and the depth of her experience carries the interest on through all improbability.

There are other devices used in achieving unity. Jane's story contains two particular periods of deep misery, which occur, first, when she is dispatched to Lowood, and, second, when she leaves Rochester. These are roughly symmetrically arranged, in such a way that her experiences of misery and joy alternate. There are also unifying parallels between Rochester and St John, between the two sets of cousins, Reeds and Riverses, and between the two uncles, Reed and Eyre. Forebodings, such as Jane feels after her 'engagement', and foreshadowings of terrible events, as in her dream of the fire at Thornfield, all contribute to the story's unity by referring back and forth. In addition, various feelings and images recur throughout the book; Jane's terror of the 'vampire', and her closeting with the bleeding Mason, repeat her childhood terror in the 'red room'; her dreams of unborn infants occur before dreadful events; Rochester's image of her as an 'elf' occurs again and again. The older Jane is also constantly reminded of the experience of the younger; Blanche's eyes remind her of Mrs Reed, and she looks round nervously for the Reeds' cane when she returns to Gateshead.

The double view-point in time is another skilful method of holding the story together. We seem to see Jane's life both as it has just occurred, and as it is recollected ten years after her marriage to Rochester. The method gives both the immediacy of the experience, and the distancing created by those ten years. Unobtrusively placed throughout the book are the comments and reflections of an author recording in retrospect; 'watches were not so common then as now' and 'now at a distance of—I will not say how many years' are among the various observations dropped lightly into the narrative.

The building and sustaining of suspense is crucial in most stories, and Charlotte worked skilfully at this aspect of her plotting. There is an awkwardness here, because in a first-person story written years afterwards the writer is obliged to conceal facts she has known long since. But again, the reader's involvement is such that Jane's artificial concealments are a small price to pay for the suspense of the narration. Many incidents and events, including Rochester's unexplained past, the noises in the attic, the enquiries made from Madeira, and the burning of Thornfield, serve to tauten the mystery, and intrigue the reader.

The tense chiefly used is that of just-after-the-present, giving the impression that the event has just occurred. Sometimes, as when Jane sees Rochester sitting on the stile, she drops into the present tense, for even greater immediacy. The coherence and credibility of the story are greatly assisted by Charlotte's precise use of time. Although there is no elaborate apparatus of dates, months and years, nothing is allowed to become vague. To take only one chapter (36), Jane leaves Moor House 'at three o'clock p.m.' on 'the first of June' and her journey back to Thornfield takes her 'six-and-thirty hours'. The spacing of months and years is unobtrusively revealed, and even minutes are sometimes precisely defined; the orderly St John allows himself fifteen minutes to dream of Rosamund Oliver, and allows Jane fifteen minutes to think over his proposal of marriage.

Themes

The chief theme of the novel is revealed as a girl's growth to mature independence, and an equal partnership in love. Jane achieves her independence by her own spirited struggle through adversity, and she understands in the end that she is her own woman and can manage her own life. Although she chooses to devote herself to Rochester, she is not dependent on him and her choice is free. Not only is she free, but in her own eyes she is eventually his equal; 'equal—as we are!' she cries, when they finally come together. The development of Jane's love for Rochester, with all it reveals of the difficulties of a satisfactory relationship in love and marriage, lies at the core of the book.

Although never doubting God's mercy, Jane does not follow her friend Helen Burns in quietly submitting to whatever fate befalls her. By her passion and her fighting spirit she demonstrates that, for her, a life of fire and feeling is preferable to a life of acceptance, or a life, like St John's, governed by reason and rectitude. The collision between feeling and reason is strong in Jane, and although in every crisis she holds to reason, this collision is the source of much of her suffering. Rochester soon observes that in her passion and judgement are at war, even if judgement always has the last word. Cold, ambitious reason is St John's chief guide, and it is unfavourably contrasted with Rochester's full-blooded involvement in life and love.

Jane's story reveals also an abiding concern with religion, and the right relation to God. Although for a while God's image is obscured by that of Rochester, through all her sufferings Jane never doubts divine mercy, even when for a brief time she finds she cannot pray. When she leaves Rochester and faces death on the moors, she turns again to God, commending Rochester and her own soul to Him. Several different attitudes to faith are exhibited and rejected; Mr Brocklehurst's cruel hypocrisy, St John's cold fanatacism, Helen's gentle acceptance, Mrs Reed's refusal to forgive, and Eliza's rigid Catholicism, are all censured in various forms, fiercely, gently, or covertly. Jane believes it is right to struggle against adversity, but hatred and revenge are not permitted. Even as a child, momentarily triumphant after her outburst against Mrs Reed, she soon regrets what she has done.

The lurid scene when she is left with the bleeding Mason, among the candle-lit panels of the apostles, may be taken as an emblem of the struggle for her soul. Luke, representing God, and Judas, in the role of Satan, seem to bear down on her until she is terrified. The scene carries hints of the great challenge about to come, when she must either reject her love, or her conscience and her God.

Throughout the story there is a clear identification between plainness and warmth on the one hand, and beauty and coldness on the other. Jane is continually described as plain, both by herself and others, and in spite of his darkness and flashing eyes, Rochester is evidently far from handsome. The only truly handsome creature in the book is Rivers, and he lacks humanity and warmth. The theme is common to almost all Charlotte's work, and seems to have meant more to her than a mere repudiation of convention.

The characters

Jane: Jane and Lucy Snowe (V), the heroines with whom Charlotte most fully identified, are the most complex, rounded, and convincing of her characters. A narrator in the first person has a problem in conveying his or her appearance. Charlotte uses various devices for overcoming this difficulty; Jane's appearance is gradually revealed through her own self-deprecating comments, her descriptions of what she sees in the mirror, and the words other people use of her. When she is a child, the Reeds' housekeeper Abbot sees her as 'a little toad', and Mrs Reed finds her expression 'scheming'. Jane has no illusions about her own looks. She believes she is plain, unattractive, and without charm. Even after Rochester has fallen in love with her, she still believes, when she rejects St John, that no-one could wish to marry her for love. One of Charlotte's skills lies in indicating how Jane under-estimates both her looks and her charm. Almost as soon as she arrives at Thornfield, Rochester begins his many references to her as an 'elf' and a 'phantom', indicating lightness and grace, and later, after his proposal, he finds her blooming, with rosy lips and radiant eyes. Although not beautiful, she is obviously better-looking than she thinks. As for her personality, it charms all but the Reeds and the Brocklehursts. Her headmistress and Helen Burns, Rochester and Adèle and Mrs Fairfax, and the Rivers family all find her lovable.

She is, however, by no means merely a sweet girl. Much of the interest of her character rises from the inner conflict between her powerful emotions and her respect for conscience and reason. She finds this conflict painful, and cannot easily resolve it. As she says of herself in relation to St John, she knows no way between 'absolute submission and determined revolt'; it is part of her growth that in the end, in her relation with Rochester, she finds a balance between the two. There are other enlivening contrasts in her nature, between her humility and her pride, her self-criticism and her self-respect, her sweetness and her strength.

Emotion is always trembling just below the surface, although it is not exposed for all to see. Rochester, in his guise as a gypsy, remarks on her reserve, and it is a long time before she reveals her feelings to him. Even as a small child she has strong passions, and when she cannot contain them any longer they explode against the Reeds. She can barely raise the courage to leave Thornfield, but somehow she finds the resolution to go. Her iron control is in fact equal to the task of curbing her passions. In her two cruellest tests—the abandoning of Rochester, and the rejection of the hypnotic power of St John—she reveals her strength. Above all she is directed by what Rochester perceives as 'that still small voice which interprets the dictates of conscience'. Right action matters greatly to her; after she has left Thornfield she feels that God directed her to the 'correct choice', and she was right to reject the temptation of 'a frenzied moment'.

Jane sees marriage as based on romantic love, a radiant emotion which so idolises the beloved that God himself is obscured. Her passion for Rochester reveals itself in trembling and flushing, and she is apprehensive about the strength of her own feelings. She rebuffs his advances, refuses to be treated to jewels and riches, and refuses to become his mistress; yet she feels intensely for him, and on one occasion finds that 'the crisis was perilous; but not without its charm'. She understands, simply and without guile, how to keep his emotions simmering by 'the pleasure of vexing and soothing him by turns'. When they are married she sees herself fulfilled as 'bone of his bone and flesh of his flesh'. Although to today's reader her words seem so guarded, Charlotte never wrote so frankly again; critics accused her of coarseness and crudity, and the attack went deep.

Jane is open to the guidance of dreams, intuitions, and psychic events, and her life is full of them. Before the news of the Reeds' disasters, and before her first 'wedding', she dreams of an infant; she dreams of the burning of Thornfield before she hears of it; she dreams of her mother bidding her to 'flee temptation'. At Lowood she is mysteriously moved to advertise as a governess; she has forebodings that she will not become Mrs Rochester. And she is in telepathic communion with Rochester, who hears her cry from the Riverses' house in response to his own call. Her own words on presentiments and 'sympathies', just before she is summoned to the Reeds, describe her belief in these inexplicable psychic events.

Jane shows marked courage from childhood onwards, and it rarely deserts her. Her spirit is indomitable; it sustains her through Brocklehurst's bullying, it enables her to withstand Rochester's arrogant demands, and it wavers only momentarily under the pressure of St John. Her spirit is matched by her physical courage: she quenches the fire in Rochester's bed; she endures her long solitude with the wounded Mason; cold and starving, she battles across the moors.

She describes herself as a free being with an independent will, and even her love of Rochester does not lead her to abandon this fierce independence. Because she prefers to support herself in the period of her engagement, she will not accept Rochester's luxurious gifts, and she will not give up her post as Adèle's governess. She is pleased with the independence she achieves through her little school at Morton, and she is unashamedly proud of her achievements in learning; to Hannah at Moor House she describes herself as 'a good scholar'. She also takes pleasure in her skill as an artist, and enjoys the tributes of Rochester and the Riverses. The idea of a small inheritance, which will establish her independence, is tempting, and she regrets Mrs Reed's betrayal. When such an inheritance does arrive, she is delighted, even though she keeps only a quarter for herself.

Generosity of heart and generosity with gifts are embedded in her character. She readily forgives the odious Mrs Reed, she feels sorry for the heartless Blanche, she is loving to Adèle, whose presence (as the supposed daughter of Rochester's French mistress) might well have upset her. When she is first engaged to Rochester, she gives all her money to a beggar.

Her honesty and candour never fail. As a child she cannot tell lies, even to please the terrifying Brocklehurst, and as an adult she is equally unable to deceive. She detests flattery, and enjoys Rochester's brusque honesty, which she returns in full measure with her 'needle of repartee'. She refuses to tell him he is handsome, and she never descends to flattery of servile responses.

Her perception of character is acute. As a child she understands the Reeds, as an adult she has no illusions about Rochester or the kind of husband he will make. She warms at once to kindly people, such as Mrs Fairfax and the Rivers sisters, she penetrates the hypocrisy of the Brocklehursts and the Ingrams; the only character which baffles her is St John's, and in her bewilderment she almost succumbs to his will.

Her awareness of social rank is sharp, and slighly distorts her vision. The disdain of the wealthy Ingrams makes her icily remote, but Rochester's smart friends are indeed too exaggerated to be altogether credible, and their conversation is stilted, arch and unconvincing. No doubt Charlotte's own experience in the houses of the well-to-do is responsible for this loss of focus. Jane takes her own gentility for granted. As she tells Mr Lloyd, she does not care for poverty, and she feels degraded when she is first confronted by the 'unmannered, rough, intractable' village girls at Morton. Her post there, she feels, is lowering rather than raising her in the social scale, but eventually she realises that the girls are 'flesh and blood', and as she perseveres she becomes fond of them. Social boundaries are very real to her, but even they may be conquered by love. Although she is 'poor, obscure, plain', she believes that in spirit she and Rochester are equals.

The change in her attitude to the Morton village girls is a small example of Jane's capacity for change and growth. Although her basic characteristics of deep feeling, strong conscience, and dogged courage vary little in the course of her story, she matures greatly as a person. The passionate child learns to control her feelings, the young woman finds the Reeds have no longer the power to hurt her. The frantic excitement of her first 'engagement', with its overtones of the Garden of Eden, sobers into a riper, profounder emotion. She has encountered terrible temptation, faced death on the moors, faced a kind of extinction in her domination by St John, and has overcome them all. At the end she emerges as her own woman, a stronger, fuller personality, who chooses marriage not because she must, but because she wants to.

Some critics believe that the five houses she inhabits each represent a new stage in her growth; Gateshead, Lowood, Thornfield, Moor

House and Ferndean are each characterised by a particular atmosphere and a particular series of events. The reader must decide whether these represent an allegorical journey or not.

Rochester: This dark, demonic hero is of a kind much beloved by the Brontës. He shares something of the power of Emily's Heathcliff (WH), and it is tempting to associate him with similar elemental forces. His ancestors are the passionate heroes of Lord Byron, and of Charlotte's own Angria (see 'Unpublished writings', pp.23–6). He is evidently not handsome, but his dark eyes flash under 'broad and jetty eyebrows', and to Jane's eye everything about his face is emphatic and strong. There are Satanic hints in his darkness, his passions, and his lurid past; he himself dramatises this aspect by describing himself as 'a fallen seraph of the abyss', and by associating his destiny with the witches in William Shakespeare's (1564–1616) *Macbeth*. His secret imprisonment of his mad wife adds considerably to the mystery which lurks about him. His life is filled with signs and portents, such as a blood-red moon, the cloven tree and the storm, and he is implicated in most of Jane's own dreams and psychic experiences. The sterner images of nature are constantly used to describe him; he is like a crag, an oak, his footprint is a hoof, his face is 'granite-hewn'. He is frequently associated with images of fire—the fire which will eventually perform the symbolic purging of his past. Everything about him, both in body and in personality, appears massive, fierce, and unshakeably strong.

Yet he is not strong. His spirit is not the equal of Jane's, and in the end even his physical strength is taken from him. In less skilled hands than Charlotte's, he could have become a stock figure of romantic melodrama (and there are moments when he trembles on the edge). To avoid this problem, Charlotte first creates him plain, then develops him as a character of some complexity, full of faults and weaknesses. When he first meets Jane, he is filled with self-disgust about his past life. Soon he realises that it is she who will regenerate him, she who will make his heart 'a shrine'. Symbolically, he leans on her arm when they first meet, and soon he is relying on her competence and courage to assist him in the fearful incidents which occur when his mad wife escapes. His observation of character is sharp, and he develops great understanding of Jane; in his guise as a gypsy he provides an acute summing-up of her character. And however he may wish it to appear to Jane, he is not deceived by Blanche's 'love'.

His defects are blatant, and even at the height of her love for him Jane makes no excuses for them. He is often morose, brusque, bullying. The habit of command does not come gracefully to him. He is deliberately cruel to Jane in flaunting his plans to marry Blanche, and in his brutal joke about sending Jane to Ireland. He lies to her about Grace Poole, and in spite of the fact that he is still married, he does all he can to gain Jane's love and commitment. He cruelly deceives her into supposing he is free to marry, and he is determined to go through with an illegal, bigamous marriage. His sacrilegious oaths at the ceremony hint again at his godless nature. Jane does not overstate when she sees him as 'hard and cynical: self-willed and resolute'.

Like her, however, he is capable of learning from experience, and he grows in stature throughout the book. Again like Jane, he grows through suffering; when all his hopes of happiness, and then his physical strength as well, are removed from him, he struggles painfully through to a gentleness and calm. When Jane finds him at Ferndean, he has come bitterly to regret his attempted bigamy. He is mellowed and chastened, and has found a new strength in submission to God's will.

St John Rivers: Rivers is a man in marked and deliberate contrast to Rochester. He is as cold, controlled, and righteous as Rochester is passionate, wayward, and flawed. Their looks, also, are in the strongest contrast. St John is tall, with a beautiful, chiselled face, as regular in feature as a Greek god's. Jane soon observes the lack of warmth in his nature. She begins to feel that he is governed entirely by reason, and driven by an ambition which he believes is given by God. She associates him with images of cold and purity—with marble, glaciers, and whiteness. 'I am cold; no fervour infects me', he tells her.

But this is far from true. Although his reserve and self-control rarely crack, Jane soon observes the turmoil of his feelings for Rosamond Oliver. He will not give way to them, because he considers her unsuitable as the wife of a missionary, but he suffers greatly, and some of the most erotic descriptions Charlotte ever wrote come from him. He has other human characteristics to which Jane warmly responds. He is considerate to the friendship of the three girls, and he finds Jane the post of teacher at Morton school. He is gentle in breaking the news of her legacy and their kinship, and in no way encourages her to share her fortune with his family.

Jane is horrified, however, by his belief that love is not necessary in marriage, for to her love and marriage are indissoluble. To her his view of marriage is a kind of sacrilege, while to him it is a duty in the service of God. The ruthless force of his character is such that Jane begins to waver, and believe she ought to accept his proposal. His moral pressure places her in 'an iron shroud' and under 'a freezing spell', and his kiss becomes a seal on her fetters. He is merciless in his determination to take her to India as his wife, and stonily rebuffs her attempts at friendly reconciliation. Unscrupulously, he practices a kind of hypnotism on her, and she is almost on the point of surrender 'down the torrent of his will' when she is saved by Rochester's cry.

Jane does not care for St John's preaching, which reveals his belief in a harsh, unforgiving God. And she is greatly shaken when he asserts, during a Bible-reading, that she is destined for hell. His description of his desire to enlist under the banner of 'my king, my law-giver, my captain' is couched in severe military terms. Twice Jane compares him to a tall column, which recalls her childhood image of Mr Brocklehurst as a 'black pillar'. She continues to correspond with St John after her marriage, and is impressed by his devotion as a missionary, which will soon end in death. The final paragraphs of the book are devoted to him.

The contrasts and parallels with Rochester are revealing of both men, and of Jane. Looking back, she writes 'I was a fool both times'— once for being tempted to flout her conscience, and once for nearly making a terrible error in accepting St John. Both men are unscrupulous in their wish to gain possession of her, and give little thought to her happiness. There is a grim, ironic humour in the contrast between the coldness of St John, whom the world would consider a good man, and the impulsive warmth of Rochester, whom the world would hold to be a wicked one.

Structurally the parallels between Rochester and St John give shape and contrast to Jane's story. There is also a unifying parallel between the two sets of cousins, Reeds and Riverses, and perhaps also between the crude bullying of John Reed (who dies young of his dissipations), and the more sophisticated pressures of St John (who dies young in the service of his God).

Some minor characters: Mrs Reed is a study in self-righteous malevolence. She finds the young Jane a 'tiresome ill-conditioned child', and is unnerved by Jane's wary watchfulness. Although she pampers her own children, she shows no kindness to Jane, who has to eat alone, and for her outburst is locked in the 'red room'. When Jane is dispatched to Lowood, Mrs Reed undermines her further by telling Mr Brocklehurst that she is a liar. She tells Jane's uncle that Jane is dead, because she does not intend that her niece should receive any inheritance. When she is dying, she confesses what she has done, but shows little remorse. She cannot forgive Jane's childhood outbursts, and feels that Jane must take the responsibility for any wrong that she herself has done. She wishes for no reconciliation, and dies hating Jane. Her greedy, vicious son John, who bullied Jane mercilessly when they were children, becomes a wastrel and eventually kills himself. His sister Eliza grows up cold and puritanical, becomes a nun and then the Superior of her convent. The spoiled, golden-haired Georgiana grows fat and lazy; she is insolent to Jane when she returns to Gateshead, and wishes she could be spared the trouble of her mother's death.

Mr Brocklehurst is probably the most menacing and evil of all Charlotte's characters. The young Jane first sees him as a black pillar towering over her, with a 'grim face at the top . . . like a carved mask'. Although professing the Christian faith, he deals in terror and cruelty, threatening Jane with hell-fire and castigating her as a liar and a servant of the Devil. He keeps the girls at Lowood so short of food and warmth that they become ill, he refuses to allow them ornaments or even to have curly hair, and he decks his own well-fed family in frills and furs. His rule of terror is so intimidating that only Miss Temple, his superintendent, has the courage to brave his displeasure.

Miss Temple is the first person (apart from the Reeds' servant Bessie) to show Jane any consistent kindness. Her fire, and the cake she offers, symbolise an affection Jane has never known before. Miss Temple is a handsome woman, and a good teacher, who elicits interest and corrects gently. She has the boldness to defy Mr Brocklehurst by replacing the girls' burnt porridge with bread and cheese. When she leaves to marry, Jane does not wish to remain at Lowood any longer.

Helen Burns is the only pupil at Lowood for whom Jane feels real affection, but when Jane arrives Helen is already ill with tuberculosis. She is clever, affectionate, and endlessly forbearing, even of the most unjust punishment. She faces her oncoming death with a calm acceptance of God's will, and she dies in Jane's arms. Jane, with her fighting spirit, admires but cannot sympathise with Helen's docile acceptance. Only much later in her story, when she leaves Rochester and commends herself to God, can she begin to understand Helen's philosophy.

Blanche Ingram is a shallow, vivacious beauty who is determined to capture the wealthy Mr Rochester. He encourages her hopes in order to arouse Jane's jealousy, but he knows she does not love him. In spite of her pain, Jane finds it impossible to be jealous of Blanche, because she is so contemptible. They are two totally contrasted women, one beautiful, the other plain; one rich, the other poor; one shallow, the other deep and complex.

Style and imagery

At its best, Charlotte's writing is eloquent and dynamic, with a confident congruence between word, thought, and feeling. But it is powerful, rather than polished, and forged rather than facile. Although she enjoys the sweep of long sentences, her style of punctuation, using many colons, breaks them up into manageable lengths, and they are often (though less often than in *Shirley*) interspersed with shorter lines.

The vigour of her prose comes in part from her use of strong, vivid verbs; in one brief passage (Chapter 4) Jane is 'hauled' to wash, has a scrubbing 'inflicted' on her, has her hair 'disciplined', is 'denuded' of her pinafore, and 'bid' to go downstairs. But above even her use of verbs stands Charlotte's precise, concrete imagery. It is this which gives her style its force, and which gives the best of her writing the concentration of poetry. In this respect her prose is more 'poetic' than most of her verse (see 'The poems' p.91). Much of the imagery is drawn from the elements, especially fire and water. Rochester is frequently associated with fire; images of flood and rising water come readily to Jane when she is in trouble—the night she parts with Rochester she hears 'a flood loosened in remote mountains'. Another fruitful source of imagery is the natural world of landscape and weather. Jane's most terrible moment of suffering is expressed in the passage beginning 'A Christmas frost had come at midsummer' (Chapter 26). Trees and wind are often invoked; after the 'engagement' the chestnut writhes and groans, and the wind roars. The moon is observed, especially in connection with Rochester, sometimes red 'as a hot cannon ball', sometimes cold and stony. As a child, Jane sees her anger with Mrs Reed like 'a ridge of lighted heath, alive, glancing, devouring'; Rochester is seen as granite and as a crag; St John is described in terms of frost, iron and stone; and when she hears about Céline, Jane feels in her heart 'the green snake of jealousy, rising on undulating coils'. The imagery is frequently condensed into vivid metaphor; Mr Brocklehurst is a 'black pillar', and St John a 'white column'.

Images of nature are often used to point a mood. Scene, season, and feeling fuse in such a way that each penetrates and reinforces the other. At the beginning of the book the clouds are 'sombre', the rain 'penetrating', and the shrubbery 'leafless'. At once the way is prepared for the introduction of Jane's misery. In all Charlotte's books the various stages of the story are set firmly in their seasons, with a strong feeling for the effects of warmth and cold, and *Jane Eyre* is no exception.

Another of Charlotte's skills lies in the indirect conveyance of information, so avoiding much verbose description; John Reed's cruel teasing of Jane, for instance, indicates without any comment that she is alone, without adult protection, and without standing in the family.

Charlotte, however, does not always write well. She was notoriously obstinate in not revising what she had written (see 'Writings', pp.32–40), and sometimes her prose is ponderous and overblown. Occasionally she reveals a weakness for over-long sentences, for obscure words (such as 'hebdomodal'), and for high-flown rhetoric. When Rochester says 'Your pity . . . is the suffering mother of love: its anguish is the very natural pang of the divine passion' a false note is sounded. Indeed her passages of conversation often sound stilted; the interchanges between the Ingrams in particular are so arch and formal as to be barely credible. It often appears that she did not have so accurate an ear for speech as her sisters.

Charlotte has a habit in all her novels of breaking her narrative in order to address her readers directly. It is often done with a quiet intimacy, and has a double effect; on the one hand, it draws the reader's sympathy by seeming to confide, and on the other it distances the narrative by breaking and intruding. Often it is effective, as when Jane is in pain or in danger, but sometimes it is used merely to draw up the threads of the plot. Charlotte's most celebrated and quoted sentence is probably, 'Reader, I married him'.

Symbolism

This is probably the richest in symbols of all Charlotte's novels. So much that happens relates to two kinds of experience, subjective and objective, that some critics have been tempted to see the whole book as a symbol of the soul's journey. The splitting of the chestnut-tree on the night of the betrothal, and the tearing of the wedding-veil, are clearly symbols of Jane's coming severance with Rochester. The firing of Rochester's bed seems at first merely an act of vengeance by Bertha, but its symbolic nature is revealed when Bertha chooses Jane's bed to start the fire that burns down Thornfield. The destruction of Rochester's home is not only an act of arson, it is also a fire of purgation, a symbol for the regeneration of Rochester through the obliteration of his past, and the destruction of his crude physical strength.

On the midsummer evening of the betrothal, the garden at Thornfield is identified with Eden, not only in its radiance but in the temptation Jane unwittingly presents to Rochester. Ferndean, on the other hand, lost in a dank wilderness, indicates the loss of paradise, which has vanished for Rochester in the loss of Jane and of his physical wholeness. Ferndean is not redeemed until Jane comes. Then it becomes a home where love and reality prevail; the exaggerated passions and the nightmare memories of Thornfield can be forgotten. Rochester's suffering through maiming and blindness is paralleled by Jane's suffering on the moors beyond Whitcross. Her cold and hungry wanderings stand as a sign for her loss of direction in life, and her loss of warmth and love. The name of the village, Whitcross, where she is put down on the edge of the moors, contains hints of the cold and holy life she is to encounter in St John.

It may also be thought (see 'Writings', pp.32–40) that the five houses in which Jane lives (Gateshead, Lowood, Thornfield, Moor House, and Ferndean) bear a symbolic relation to her life. Each marks new experiences, and each creates new challenges which evoke new responses. Each is associated with a prevailing colour; Gateshead with red, Lowood with grey, Thornfield with snow and fire. Moor House is touched with the whiteness of St John, and Ferndean is buried in a green gloom. In the course of her passage through these five houses, Jane grows up.

Charlotte as Jane Eyre

Jane tells her story as her own autobiography, but a part of it is also based on the life of her creator. The descriptions of Lowood, and even of friends and teachers, correspond closely to Charlotte's own schooling at the Clergy Daughters' School (see 'Life', pp.27–31); and Jane's experience with the Ingrams, showing the kind of treatment a governess could expect, is based on Charlotte's personal knowledge. Reconstructions of various small events in her life are scattered through the book; the firing of Rochester's bed echoes an episode in Branwell's life; Bewick's *British Birds* was a favourite on the shelves at Haworth; the confinement of a mad woman in an attic was a story Charlotte had heard at Stonegappe.

It is also clear, from all we know of Charlotte's thoughts and feelings, that Jane's character is a close reflection of her own. Her painful conviction of her own lack of beauty, her views on love and marriage, her motherless state, her high intelligence, and her perseverance in adversity are all traits she shares with her heroine. But the fact that so much is drawn from Charlotte's life does not detract from the achievement of the book. Her creative intensity is such that all the material, real and invented, is equally fused into the stuff of her story.

The reception of *Jane Eyre*

The book appeared under the name of Currer Bell, and no-one outside Charlotte's immediate family knew if this was man or woman. By and large, Charlotte was fortunate in her reviews, and certainly more fortunate than Emily and Anne two months later. Several critics admired the novel's vigour, style, freshness, and understanding of character. G.H. Lewes, the perceptive critic who later became a friend of Charlotte's, welcomed it as 'Decidedly the best novel of the season', commended its semblance of reality, and hoped for more books from Currer Bell. Two years later, reviewing *Shirley*, he referred back to *Jane Eyre* as 'a work of . . . power, piquancy, and originality.' But he did also remark that its vigour 'often amounts to coarseness', and this distressed Charlotte. Although she disdained all that was foolishly genteel or refined, she strongly upheld decorum.

The attacks in the *Christian Remembrancer* also emphasised the masculine coarseness of the writing, which was considered especially objectionable as the book appeared to be the work of a woman. *The Quarterly Review* led the fiercest of the attacks, holding that the novel breathed social revolution, challenged God's proper ordering of rich and poor, and encouraged 'ungodly discontent'. This seems an over-reaction to Charlotte's modest plea for the place of women, and the power of love, but it angered and hurt her, and she answered it with *Shirley*.

Shirley

Summary

When three loquacious curates of West Yorkshire meet for an evening meal, they are interrupted by Matthewson Helstone, the masterful parson of Briarfield, who tells them that Hollow's Mill (which is man-aged by Robert Moore) is in danger of attack by the workers. The men bitterly resent the new machinery which is taking their jobs away from them. Moore lives near the mill, with his sister Hortense, and rents it from its owner, the young Shirley Keeldar of Fieldhead. Trade is bad, and he faces bankruptcy.

News comes that his machines have been smashed on the way to the mill, and Moore and Helstone set out to rescue the men who were accompanying them. They encounter Mr Yorke, who had found the wounded men on the moor, and he invites the party to his fine house, Briarmains. Hiram Yorke (once the guardian of Shirley) is a prosper-ous, radical Yorkshireman, highly cultivated but blunt in manner. He and his formidable wife, Hester, have a family of five lively children.

The next morning Caroline Helstone, who lives with her uncle, arrives at the Moores' cottage for a French lesson with Hortense. She delights in Robert's company, and is apprehensive of the dangers he runs. She is a pretty, gentle girl of eighteen, who had been taken from her mother as an infant, and had lost her dissolute father (Helstone's brother) when a child. Robert treats her with affection, but he begins to feel this is a weakness and must be stopped. Caroline now realises she loves Robert, and her heart soars; but the next day Robert is brusque, and in great anguish she realises she must subdue her feelings.

At the mill the next day Robert receives a deputation of unemployed workmen whose leader is Moses Barraclough, a Methodist preacher, who had led the attack on the machinery. The brazen Barraclough is arrested, but one of the group, William Farren, makes a plea for their starving families, only to be harshly rebuffed by Moore. Back in his bare cottage, Farren is visited by the kindly Mr Hall, vicar of a nearby parish, who offers him a loan. In the evening Moore visits the Yorke family, and asks Yorke if he will employ Farren as a gardener.

Like most businessmen, Moore wants an end to war with France, and he quarrels publicly with Helstone. As a result (and also because he suspects a mutual affection) Helstone forbids Caroline to visit the Moores. She submits, as her visits there are now acutely painful, and feels she must face the prospect of never marrying. She reflects on the sad state of unmarried women, and decides to visit the two local spinsters, Miss Mann and Miss Ainley. They are plain but engaging women, and their example determines Caroline to fill her days with visits, walks, sewing, and studies. Even so, she is filled with despair and wanders out at night to gaze at Robert's lighted window. She suggests to her uncle that she should seek a place as a governess, but he dismisses the idea with horror.

One day, when she has become thin and ill, he takes her to meet Shirley Keeldar, who has arrived to live at her great house, Fieldhead. A matronly woman, Mrs Pryor, enters the parlour, and Caroline feels drawn to her. Shirley arrives, graceful and at ease, and introduces Mrs Pryor as her governess. Spiritedly she describes her task as captain of her inheritance, and talks with interest to Caroline, who is shy but attracted.

Caroline begins to visit Fieldhead often, enjoying the company of Mrs Pryor as well as that of Shirley, but she is made uneasy by Shirley's frequent references to Robert. One night she sees Shirley and Robert talking softly together. She feels doomed, and convinced they will marry. More than ever she wishes to leave and become a governess, but Mrs Pryor warns her against such a desolate life. Moore arrives to tell Shirley of his plans to prevent further attacks on the mill, and Caroline, suffering in the shadows, sees how Shirley admires him. When Shirley next visits Briarfield, Caroline tells her why she is so wretched.

Shirley feels that, as a local proprietor, she must help the poor of the district. They ask Miss Ainley's help, and Shirley donates three hundred pounds to the new charitable fund. When it is distributed the neighbourhood becomes calmer. But Moore is pressed by financial problems, and still expects an attack on his mill. He hints of his growing feeling for Shirley. At the Whit-Tuesday parish feast the procession of parishioners and bands march off to the Common, but they encounter, head on, another procession made up of local Dissenters. Helstone's determination disperses the Dissenters, and their procession collapses.

Shirley lyrically describes to Caroline her vision of 'my mother Eve', but Caroline longs only for her own mother. They encounter Farren, who warns them of a general hatred of Moore in the neighbourhood. Moore's foreman joins them, and asserts that women should follow their men's opinions, but Shirley confounds him with her knowledge of public affairs.

Helstone has to be away for the night, and he asks Shirley to stay with Caroline at Briarfield, and gives her his pistols. Soon after midnight the girls hear marching men, and Shirley persuades the trembling Caroline to run with her to the mill to give warning. From a vantage-point on top of a hill, they see the rioters are already assembled in front of the mill, and Caroline wishes to rush to help Robert. But Shirley restrains her, pointing out that this is 'a struggle about money, and food, and life'. When the rioters break into the yard and shoot, the fire is returned and a confused battle ensues. But Moore and his men are well organised, and at dawn the rioters withdraw. The girls see Robert in the yard, and again Shirley has to restrain Caroline from running to him.

After a rest back at Briarfield, Shirley determines to ask Robert why he did not tell her the attack was coming—'Men,' she cries, 'fancy women's minds something like those of children'. At Fieldhead Shirley gives orders for food and medicines to be sent in quantities to the wounded men. When Moore arrives, returning the over-supply, Helstone praises his generalship. He also defends himself from Yorke's strictures on his behaviour as a parson, and on Moore's heartless behaviour to his workers. After Shirley's outburst in Moore's defence, Yorke coyly asks when the wedding is to be, but is treated with disdain. On a walk Mrs Pryor tells Caroline of her early trials as a governess, and reflects bitterly on the difficulties of marriage. She offers Caroline a place with her when Shirley marries, and Caroline is much moved.

Moore sets out to hunt down the riot leaders, and puts himself in great danger. His business is on the point of ruin, and all summer he scarcely sees Caroline or Shirley. Shirley's prim, conventional uncle, Mr Sympson, arrives at Fieldhead with his family. Caroline's visits there are much curtailed, and she sinks into deep dejection. One day Hortense sends a secret note asking Caroline to visit her. She is delighted to be in Robert's cottage again, and she lingers on, hoping he will come. Eventually he arrives with his brother Louis, so like him that Caroline is confused. Louis is the tutor of Henry, Mr Sympson's son, and has come north to join the family.

At home again, Caroline develops a fever which will not abate. Mrs Pryor comes to stay, and nurses her lovingly. Caroline rouses herself only on Tuesdays, when Robert rides by on the road to market. Unaware of what she is doing, she cries out for him, feeling she is going to die. Eventually, tremulously, Mrs Pryor tells Caroline she is her mother. She relates her terrible history, and Caroline embraces her fervently. Even the flinty Helstone is moved to see their happiness, and Caroline's recovery begins.

Visiting Fieldhead, Caroline meets the correct and decorous Sympsons, and their lame little son Henry, who is a clever and unusual child. She finds Louis an impressive figure, but silent and reserved. She observes with surprise that Shirley ignores and denigrates him, and is irritable in his presence. One day, when Caroline is alone with Henry, the boy finds a packet of French essays in Louis' desk, and Caroline is astonished to see that they were written by Shirley four years before. When she arrives, Shirley snatches them away, and does not explain.

Mr Sympson is outraged when Shirley refuses proposals of marriage from four eligible young men, including the amiable Sir Philip Nunnely. She asserts she will marry only for love. When Louis is ill, Shirley creeps upstairs to see him, but he believes she is encouraging Nunnely and rebuffs her. When he is better, he asks her to come and read to him in the school-room, and their uneasiness slowly alters to a warm accord.

Shirley begins to look ill, and Henry tells Louis she has made her will. Louis now recognises his love for her, but rejects it as hopeless. When she arrives she shows him a deep scar on her arm, which had been caused by a mad dog, and which she had cauterised herself with a hot iron. He calms her fear of rabies, and obliquely confesses his love. Alone on a winter night, he passes the time in Shirley's study, writing of her passionate character and the history of his love, which he believes can never be fulfilled.

At last Robert returns from London, where he has been securing the conviction of the rioters. Yorke meets him on the moor, and Robert reveals that he had proposed to Shirley before he went away, and had been angrily rejected. He acknowledges now that he was attracted by her wealth, and had never loved her. Since he has been away he has seen great misery, and he vows to become a more compassionate man. As Yorke rides on, he hears a shot.

During an irascible interview with her uncle, Shirley asserts that for a husband she requires a master. Louis enters, with the news that Robert has been shot, and is in danger. After the shooting Yorke had taken him to Briarmains for nursing. Louis is allowed to see him, but Shirley and Caroline are not. For a time death is near, but soon the danger passes, and Caroline longs to visit him. One winter evening Yorke's son, Martin, encounters Caroline, and mischievously tells her that Robert will die. Intrigued by her horror, he arranges that one evening everyone at Briarmains will be out of the way, and takes Caroline up to Robert's sick-room. She and Robert now discover how much they have longed to meet, and when Caroline makes plain her love he promises atonement if he lives. When he eventually returns to his cottage, he and Caroline spend an evening of great happiness. He confesses his mercenary proposal to Shirley, and discovers from Caroline that Shirley loves Louis.

Louis again writes in his journal, describing how he contrived to be alone with Shirley. Both fraught and uneasy, they converse obliquely for a long time, until Louis no longer feels barred by her wealth and declares his love. In the end she capitulates, and they pledge themselves to one another. Mr Sympson bursts in, and becomes apoplectic with rage, and Louis attacks and almost strangles him. He then resigns his tutorship and finds employment in nearby Stillboro'.

Robert has decided to pursue his attacker no further. Trade with America is now permitted, and his business begins to flourish again. At last he feels he can ask Caroline to marry him. They ask Caroline's mother to live with them, and they will continue to live in the same parish as Shirley and Louis. The two couples are married in a double wedding, and in the following years industry and prosperity come to the Hollow.

The writing of *Shirley*

Charlotte was writing this novel in 1848–9, one of the most terrible periods in her life, during which Branwell, Emily and Anne all died. She found work was the only cure for 'rooted sorrow', and she finished the book in time for publication in the autumn of 1849. The criticism of *Jane Eyre* as anti-Christian and revolutionary, as well as coarse, spurred her to try to demonstrate that people could be questioning, compassionate, and poor, without being ungodly anarchists. She had also taken to heart the words of G.H. Lewes, who had advised her to avoid melodrama, and to make use of her own experience. She wished now to explore an altogether different world from that of *Jane Eyre*. Reverting again to what she had attempted in *The Professor*, she put romance behind her, and on the first page of her new book warned the reader that it was to be 'unromantic as Monday morning'.

Plot and structure

For all its awkward corners, the plotting is more realistic than that of *Jane Eyre*. It is set in 1812, in the year of a major Luddite rising, and it is firmly embedded in its historical background, with many references to the Napoleonic wars (see 'Historical Background', pp.5–11) and the trading problems of the time. It does not turn on improbabilities, psychic events, or Gothic mysteries. It is, as Charlotte described it, 'real, cool and solid', with all wilder flights of the imagination set aside. The four houses on which the story centres—Briarfield, Field-head, Briarmains, and Hollow's Mill cottage—are all close together, and for the most part their inhabitants meet and part and meet again as real people in real life. Their stories are interwoven naturally, without contrivance, and even the surprising re-entry of Louis into Shirley's life is arranged without awkwardness.

However, when G.H. Lewes came to review *Shirley* in the *Edinburgh Review* in 1850, he expressed the view that Charlotte had never made up her mind just what kind of book she had wanted to write. Was it, he asked, a regional novel of Yorkshire during the Luddite riots, or was it a character study, or was it a love story? Although there were many aspects of the book he admired, he saw it as a series of random sketches, many of them brilliant, but never amounting to a coherent book.

Few have disagreed with his view that the structure is deeply flawed. The story falls awkwardly into two parts, with the heroine of the title not appearing until a third of the way through. Even then Caroline retains a rôle as significant as Shirley's, and her character throughout is more convincingly analysed than her friend's. If they are intended as joint heroines, the rôle does not sit easily on either. Charlotte was in much doubt about what to call the book, and this may well reveal her own uncertainties about it. She first thought of 'Hollow's Mill', then eventually left it to her publisher to decide between 'Fieldhead' and 'Shirley'. Something of her uneasiness in presenting two heroines is reflected in the handling of the two Moore brothers. While Robert is clearly of greater importance in the structure of the story, he is nevertheless almost entirely displaced in the last few chapters by Louis.

At first the interest seems to centre on Dissent and industrial unrest, but this theme soon gives way to the lives and loves of Caroline and Shirley, and reappears only intermittently thereafter. There is in fact no dominating interest capable of unifying the story, just as there is no dominating character to capture and sustain sympathy.

This is the only novel in which Charlotte takes the part of omniscient narrator, and she appears to have found it less congenial than writing in the first person. The choice also deprived her of the unifying effect provided by a first-person narrative. But even in her rôle as objective narrator, she does not hold consistently to one viewpoint; although she is not writing directly in the first person, she presents a considerable part of the story through Caroline's eyes. And towards the end, further disrupts the narrative viewpoint by revealing Louis' love largely through the pages of his own journal.

The action is often interrupted by long passages, of interest in themselves, but largely irrelevant to the story unfolding around them. The detailed analysis of the Yorke family, however entertaining and acute, has little bearing on the development of the book; so too, the lengthy introduction of the curates, and the later descriptions of the Whitsun celebrations, outweigh their relevance and outlast their interest. Charlotte enjoyed the creation of 'set pieces', and when she is describing Malone's pursuit of Caroline at tea, or the Misses Ainley and Mann, her proportions are skilfully judged. But many of the longer scenes create too great an imbalance. The story is also overburdened with minor characters, who may interest or amuse, but are not integrated sufficiently into the plot. The Yorkes, Malone, and even Mrs Pryor are presented in more detail than their places in the story merit.

If the binding links are tenuous, they are nevertheless there. The love-story of Caroline runs almost from beginning to end of the novel, and many of the events are given unity by being presented from her point of view. So too, Robert's comings and goings, as he pursues both his public and his private life, span much of the book and link many of its episodes. And Helstone is seldom absent from the scene for long. Various mysteries, such as Shirley's unexplained illness and the obscurity surrounding Mrs Pryor, also help to impel the story forward by maintaining suspense. The confined area of a few square miles, in which most of the characters live, has also an effect in creating a unity of place. Although Robert goes to Stillboro' and London, and Shirley to the Lake District, the story never moves away from the parish of Briarfield.

Was Lewes right in believing that Charlotte had not made up her mind what kind of novel she wished to write? It would be equally possible to believe that she had indeed made up her mind, and fully intended to write of Church and Dissent, industrial anarchy, poverty, love, marriage, and social class—but that the scheme proved too ambitious and too unsuited to her skills.

Themes

The diversity of themes may have proved difficult to organise, but it gives great richness to the book. Charlotte was boldly original in attempting an historical, regional novel, with social and economic themes. In the 1840s, when she wrote, the Chartist movement was growing, and the Luddite attacks in the early years of the century were still fresh in many minds (see 'Historical background', pp.5–11). All his life Charlotte's father carried pistols, remembering his days near Rawfold's Mill, which had been the target of a famous Luddite attack, and was the model for the attack on Hollow's Mill in *Shirley*. Charlotte's attempt to find a balance between the rights of the mill-owners and the rights of the unemployed is a central theme of the book. Sympathy for Moore, and admiration for his courage, are balanced by sympathy for Farren and his fellows, and appreciation of the practical kindness of Mr Hall. At the beginning Moore regards the rioters as 'vermin', but his own later experience, and Caroline's persuasion, lead him to regret his harshness and to 'give better wages . . . do some good'.

The opposition between the mills which will bring prosperity, and the great natural beauty they will destroy, is left unresolved, and hangs as an awkwardness between Caroline and Robert as they begin their married life. He will fill the green hollow with cottages, cut down the copse, and make a 'cinder-black highway'. But Caroline protests, hating the thought that the smoke of Stillboro' will fill 'the blue hill-country air', and destroy the valley that old Martha remembers as 'a bonnie spot—full of oak-trees and nut-trees'. Robert has his way, but at the end of the book Charlotte speaks in her own voice, grieving for the loss. As the book contains little of the natural imagery which came so readily to her, this protest is especially telling.

Problems of women's rights, and their place in love and marriage, are much to the fore in *Shirley*. Joe Scott, Moore's foreman, puts the case for male domination in asserting that women should reflect the opinions of their husbands, and in their spirited protests Shirley and Caroline put the case for the independent woman. Shirley is fortunate in being an heiress with property to manage, but Caroline is driven into a painful confrontation with her uncle when she wishes to gain her independence as a governess. She pities girls who do nothing but wait around for marriage, which may prove loveless, and she works at her books in an attempt to avoid that fate. Although she admires the courage of the spinsters, Miss Ainley and Miss Mann, she is painfully aware of their loneliness and poverty. When she cries, 'Men of England! look at your poor girls ... ' (Chapter 22) she is speaking in the voice of the author. She does not question that a loving marriage is the highest good (although Shirley seems much less sure); but marriage must be for love, not position, and no girl should be driven to seek it because without it she will be nothing.

Charlotte never underestimates the power of love. In all her novels it overcomes formidable barriers of religion, wealth and rank, and endures through hopelessness and pain. Caroline's despair reduces her to serious illness, yet her love for Robert is so deep she readily forgives his long neglect, and even his proposal to Shirley. Shirley is less confident about love. She feels that passion may be no more than 'a mere fire of dry sticks, blazing up and vanishing'. In this, as in much else, she seems to speak for Charlotte herself, who in 1840 expressed the same idea in a letter to Mary Taylor. Although Shirley loves Louis, and recognises him as 'my superior', she puts their wedding off again and again, and he sees that she is unwilling to lose her freedom. She cannot solve the vexing question of how a woman may retain her independence within the bonds of marriage. The master/pupil relation, so marked between her and Louis, is a formula to which Charlotte returns in every novel, trying to find in it a possible solution.

The novel's two chief love-stories are entwined with other loves and marriages, past and present. Although it must be assumed that the marriages of Shirley and Louis, and Caroline and Robert, will be happy, happy marriages in *Shirley* are few and far between. Mrs Pryor's marriage was disastrous, Helstone had made his wife wretched, Yorke married Hester only because he was jilted elsewhere, and Hester's views on marriage are briskly cynical. With the exception of Louis, the husbands and the men in love do not behave well; Robert proposes to Shirley for reasons of business, and the curate Malone sees no disgrace in pursuing marriage for wealth.

The book opens with a chapter on the curates Malone, Sweeting, and Donne, and throughout the theme of religion and the Church is never far away. In castigating Yorke for his reforming zeal, Shirley also castigates the curates for their pettiness, their self-importance, and their servility to the rich. Helstone is conscientious but, in marked contrast to his colleague Mr Hall, he is hard and overbearing. Hall, who is admired by both Shirley and Caroline, is held up as the model parish priest, concerned for the poor and ready with practical help. In her capacity as narrator, Charlotte makes clear her dislike of the High Church 'Puseyites' (see 'Religion and the Church', pp.15–17), and her abhorrence of Roman Catholicism. The Dissenters, led by the Methodist Barraclough, are at the root of the Luddite attacks, and their followers are held up to ridicule in the episode of the clashing Whitsun processions. The implication is always that, although the Church of England may be in great need of reform, the people would be badly off without its hard-working parish priests.

In all her novels Charlotte shows herself sharply aware of class structure, in its relation both to rank and to wealth. Her own experience as a governess left her with a hostile contempt for the kind of prosperous, worldly families who had employed her (see 'Life', pp.27–31). The Sympsons in *Shirley* have much in common with the Ingrams in *Jane Eyre*. Although they are presented with more wit and less caricature, their cold snobbery is no less distasteful than that of the Ingrams. Shirley resists her uncle's incredulous rage when he finds she will not marry even the wealthy Sir Philip Nunnely. Although wealthy herself, and of good social standing, she is not impressed with these attributes; she will marry only when she loves a man, of whatever rank, whom she can admire.

Charlotte also attacks another section of society, which she calls 'the mercantile classes', who clamoured for an end to the war with Napoleon and the restrictions on trade it had imposed. Robert Moore is one of those who agitate for peace, and in spite of the threat of bankruptcy he is not exonerated from the accusations of greed and selfishness.

The working-class and the poor take a significant part in this novel. As ever, Charlotte's sympathy is strong, whether for the poverty of the unemployed, such as Farren, or the genteel poverty of the Misses

Ainley and Mann. She sees no virtue in poverty, and regards it as corrosive and degrading. Yet she is no revolutionary. The workers have rights, one of which is to live warm and well-fed, but she has no sympathy for those among the Luddites and Chartists who wished to overthrow the social structure.

The characters

In her fifth chapter Charlotte tells the reader that 'every character in this book will be found to be more or less imperfect, my pen refusing to draw anything in the model line'—but adds that none will be monsters either. Her aim is to create recognisable, everyday people. In many cases she succeeds, especially with the women and some of the minor characters. Shirley and Caroline are successfully drawn, and among the minor parts Hortense, Yorke, and Helstone are vigorous and credible beings. But the heroes are less satisfactory.

Even more than usual, Charlotte has based these characters on people she knew. Many are identified in her letters, some by Mrs Gaskell, and several have been discovered since. There is a hint, when she is introducing Miss Ainley, that Charlotte prided herself on drawing from the life rather than from her imagination. Shirley herself is intended as a portrait of Emily, as she would have been had she been healthy and prosperous; Caroline is based on an amalgam of Anne, and Charlotte's friend, Ellen Nussey; the Yorke family is drawn from another set of friends, the Taylors; Hortense from a teacher in Brussels.

Shirley: As Charlotte eventually decided the novel was to be called 'Shirley' or 'Fieldhead', presumably she saw Shirley as the chief character. The difficulty in sharing this view is that Caroline's part is much the greater; she is seldom absent from the story (until near the end), many of the events are related from her standpoint, and she is the only character whose feelings are fully analysed. However, when Shirley is also present it is she who dominates, in strength of character as well as in manner and in rank. And much of the last quarter of the book is hers. She is the only one of Charlotte's heroines who is beautiful, strong, competent, and wealthy. She is liked and loved, she is 'Captain Keeldar', and she has all she wishes.

She is drawn to those she feels to be her superior in intellect and personality—'Nothing ever charms me more than when I meet my superior,' she says. She will not accept Nunnely because he is 'not my master'. Louis is quick to realise that if he is to win her he must again subdue her into their old master/pupil relationship, and tells himself 'I *must* keep up the professor'. When to his murmur of 'My pupil' she lovingly replies 'My master', he has achieved his end. But Shirley is still baffled, like so many of Charlotte's heroines, by the proper relation between men and women. She feels that men see a good woman as 'half doll, half angel' and a bad woman as 'a fiend'. She does not flourish during the period of her engagement. Louis watches her 'pinings after virgin freedom' and she puts their wedding off week after week. Only his presence can 'make amends for the lost privilege of liberty'. After her marriage Shirley has a 'happy, glad, good-natured look'; but it is in her that Charlotte comes nearest to questioning whether marriage is compatible with a free, independent spirit.

She has physical courage and stamina. She herself cauterises the dog bite with a hot iron, and whatever activity is asked of her—whether assisting the wounded or running across the countryside—she is never weary. As brave in spirit as in body, she allows no-one to bully or over-whelm her; when Robert proposes she remains firmly loyal to Caroline, and she resists all her uncle's attempts to coerce her into marriage. She detests tyranny and injustice, she declaims on the deficiencies of the Church, and always she upholds values of sympathy and sense.

The contrast with Caroline is marked, not only in their colouring and stature, but in Caroline's quiet gentleness and Shirley's buoyant vivacity. While Caroline is often despondent, Shirley is briskly 'All right'. She is an attractive heroine, as Charlotte intended her to be, but she has an unfortunate liking for overblown poetic language. The most obvious example is her high-flown passage on Eve (Chapter 18), and in moments of anger she is also given to grandiose expressions; Mr Sympson is bewildered by the long metaphorical flight with which she dismisses him, and Moore is reprimanded as 'Lucifer—Star of the Morning!'

As we have seen, Shirley's character is loosely based on that of Emily. Her looks, her vigour, her love of poetry, and her physical courage (as in the cauterising of the arm) are all reminiscent of Charlotte's sister, but Shirley has a social competence and a worldly efficiency which do not seem to have been qualities of Emily's.

Caroline: Because much of the story is seen through her eyes, Caroline emerges as the most fully realised of all the characters in the book. Her thoughts, feelings and attitudes are divulged with an intimacy which is not given even to her co-heroine. Through her the reader looks both out and in; out to the events of her life, and inward to her own suffering. She is present either as principal or onlooker throughout much of the book, and for the greater part of that time she is suffering from the pain of unrequited love. Her early hopes of Robert are painfully quenched, and she feels as if she held 'a stinging scorpion' in her hand. Her love for Robert dominates her life, and she feels the injustice of her position as a woman. Robert is at liberty to speak of love to her, yet custom does not permit her to speak to him.

The love she believes to be growing between Robert and Shirley is an agony to her, and almost more than her health can support. So wretched does she become that her brooding nature leads her to fear of rejection by God, and eventually to illness. But she does not lack spirit. She is never cowed by Robert, and is always prepared to give him her views, even if they are critical. She blames him for his treatment of his workmen, and her reference to him as Coriolanus is not intended to be flattering. She is not endowed with Shirley's unquenchable resilience, but she does not sink into docile acceptance of her suffering. She dutifully takes up the duties of visiting and sewing suggested by Miss Ainley, and she works at her books in order to prepare herself as a governess. She feels strongly that girls should be given the opportunity of independence, and is dejected by her uncle's biting scorn of her plans.

She has never known either mother or father, for her mother disappeared when she was a baby, and her father then died. Her uncle, who has brought her up, is a good but hard man, who can offer her little companionship, and he further blights her life by forbidding her visits to the Moores' cottage. Her life is lonely until the arrival of Mrs Pryor and Shirley, for both of whom she feels an immediate affection. This loyal affection survives even her suspicions of Shirley's developing love for Robert. The discovery of her mother brings her great joy, and enables her to recover from her long, debilitating illness. In spite of her mother's dire experience, Caroline does not share Shirley's doubts about marriage. She is confident that if marriage is based on mutual love and respect it must be happy.

She is evidently liked by everyone, she has gentle manners, and (unlike most of Charlotte's heroines) she is pretty.

Robert Moore: Robert is tall and dark, with a sallow face and a slightly foreign accent. Many of the scenes in which he is involved, especially those at the mill, are among the most arresting in the book. He is a man of great courage, indifferent to danger in the defence of his mill, and in his pursuit of the rioters. His determination to install new machinery arises from his conviction that the mill will soon be bankrupt if he does not. But in bringing in his machines he is causing near-starvation among his work-force, and Caroline is distressed at his indifference to their plight. He regards the men as a 'mob', and intends to hunt down the riot leaders as if they were 'vermin'. Caroline sees something of Coriolanus in his contempt for ordinary people, and he acknowledges the charge; when she tells him he should be more considerate of his men, he makes an effort to find work for William Farren. But it is not until near the end of the story, when he has brought Barraclough to

justice, that he repents his harshness, and determines to be 'more considerate to ignorance, more forbearing to suffering'.

For much of the time he is under great stress, with his business fail-
ing fast. Not only does he press for the end of the war in order to revive
trade (an unpatriotic attitude for which he is much reviled), he regards
even Caroline and Shirley with a mercenary eye. He wishes that Helstone had given Caroline a dowry instead of building a church, and he
proposes marriage to Shirley because he needs her wealth. However,
like all Charlotte's most interesting characters, he grows through
experience, and comes deeply to regret his mercenary behaviour.

He describes himself as taciturn, phlegmatic and joyless, but Shirley's view of his character is more charitable. She tells Caroline that he
is affectionate, kind, and pleasant company. And apart from his lapse
over Shirley, of which he is thoroughly ashamed, he is indeed
affectionate and kind to Caroline, even when he is determined to put
her out of his mind. It is unfortunate for her that he is a somewhat
unperceptive man, who is slow to realise how much she loves him.

But he is not a satisfactory creation, because he does not altogether
cohere as a character; Moore the businessman and Moore the lover
never quite achieve a convincing identity.

Louis Moore: As the eventual husband of a heroine who seeks a
master, Louis suffers through his late introduction into the story. He
does not appear until the last third of the book, and he is never solidly
established. He looks very like his brother, but he is more of a scholar
and less of a man of action. Although a gentleman, he is poor, and
unhappily aware of the gulf between himself and Shirley. She, however, sees him as a man she can admire, and he finds in himself the kind
of strength that needs a spirited woman for a wife. He sees Shirley as a
lioness and leopard, and she sees him as a master to whom she could
submit. But the qualities she finds in him are stated rather than exhibited. Not until the day of their engagement does he present himself as a
master who can curb her, and as a man who can heave another bodily
out of the room.

He is kind and sympathetic to his crippled young pupil, Henry, and
he is also much loved by animals, for which he has great affection.
Both Caroline and Shirley regard this as a good sign in a man; Shirley's
cat will sit purring on his knee, and her great dog, Tartar, will lie quietly beside him, 'slobbering with exceeding affection'.

Much of the course of his love for Shirley is related in his journal, in
a language as grandiloquent as some of Shirley's own. In the same
vein, the final scenes between them are spoken in a language so stilted,
so oblique, and so arch as to be barely credible. In a letter written in
1850, Charlotte described how she had written the last third of the

novel in an 'eager, restless endeavour to combat mental sufferings that were scarcely tolerable'. It seems likely that her mind was not altogether engaged in the last quarter of her novel, and she admitted that she did no revision on it.

Matthewson Helstone: Caroline's uncle and guardian has a 'hawk's head, beak and eye', and his real vocation would have been as a soldier. He has sound qualities as a pastor and a man of action, but he is hard and domineering. He gives Caroline an awkward affection but little sympathy, and he is biting about her hopes of becoming a governess. He enjoys the company of ladies, but has cynical views on marriage. Caroline feels that if everyone followed his advice, no-one would ever marry. His wife, long dead, was a gentle girl, once beloved of Hiram Yorke, but his treatment of her was hard. Robert Moore's Whig beliefs (see 'Historical background', pp.5 – 11) and his desire to end the war, so anger the Tory Helstone that he forbids Caroline to visit the Moores' cottage, causing her great pain. His character is based on clerics known to Charlotte, and in part on her father.

Hortense Moore: It is unfortunate that Hortense vanishes so early from the story, for she is one of Charlotte's happiest minor creations. She keeps house for her brother, and is a lady very well pleased with herself, both in her housekeeping and her scholarship. She plays and sings, and teaches French to Caroline until the girl is forbidden to visit her. Many of her habits remain continental, and she is extremely industrious, forever (as Caroline observes) clearing out drawers. She mends, cleans, and cooks, but preserves her appearance with curl papers and stately gowns. Her formidable manner conceals a kind heart, and she becomes very fond of Caroline. In spite of her oddity, she is accepted as a friend by Miss Mann, and the formidable Mrs Yorke.

Hiram Yorke: Although priding himself on his Yorkshire bluntness, the owner of Briarmains has filled his house with treasures from his long European travels, during which he perfected his French and German. His relationship with Helstone is close but uneasy, for his Radical views infuriate his Tory friend. He believes Moore to be too harsh with his men, and he finds a job as gardener for the unemployed Farren. His wife and he somehow contrive to live in accord, and he is proud of his lively children. Believing Robert and Shirley to be suited, he causes much trouble by encouraging Robert to propose to her.

Other minor characters: *Shirley* is especially rich in lesser characters, although many, such as most of the Yorke family, are not strictly relevant to the story. Nevertheless, they make their mark. The Misses

Ainley and Mann are lovingly drawn; Mrs Yorke is an impressive presence; the two workmen, Joe Scott and William Farren, are solid, articulate men. Old Mr Hall, the benevolent parson, is pleasantly memorable, and the portrait of the poet, the ineffectual Sir Philip Nunnely, is delicately drawn.

Style

Much of the writing is splendidly vigorous, with the energetic drive of Charlotte at her best. Sentence-lengths are greatly varied, nouns, verbs, and phrases are pungent and condensed; the doctors attending Robert 'wrought and wrangled' over him; Caroline descends the stairs 'in a subdued flutter'; Mr Sympson is elated as 'any middencock on pattens'. There is more conversation than is usual with Charlotte, and much of it is natural and lively. The early scenes at the mill are particularly full of swift exclamation and talk. However, serious conversation round a tea-table is considerably more stilted, and the curates' discussions in the first chapter are clogged with laboured humour; although Caroline and Robert speak naturally, the conversations between Shirley and Louis do not flow easily. Both fall readily into the pseudo-poetic language which also bedevils their writing.

Charlotte's habit of addressing the reader, and of breaking into French, is given the usual scope. The desire to establish an intimacy, and to make excuses for having lost her way, are as frequent here as elsewhere. Sometimes the habit is merely an irritant, but sometimes the aside succeeds in drawing the reader closer; when Charlotte shares her pride in Yorkshire with Hiram Yorke, the effect is to bind and not to distance the reader.

Although it has strength and vigour, the writing is less delicate and less charged than in either *Jane Eyre* or *Villette*. The richness of imagery, the constant reference to the natural world, and the use of words and phrases which echo back and forth through these two novels, are markedly lacking in *Shirley*. This is no doubt deliberate, as part of the 'Monday morning' effect Charlotte was seeking, but it deprives her of one of her greatest strengths.

The reception of *Shirley*

The book did not cause the kind of stir generated by *Jane Eyre*, but the familiar charges of 'coarseness' and social anarchy came from journals such as *The Quarterly Review* and the *Christian Remembrancer—* journals dubbed by Charlotte 'those heavy Goliaths of the periodical press'. Some of the comments of G.H. Lewes have already been quoted (see 'Plot and structure', pp.66–8). He also found the novel 'over-masculine' and flippant (charges which irritated Charlotte), and he urged the author to 'discipline her . . . tumultuous energies'. But he also commented on 'power unmistakable', even if it was often undisciplined. Many literary people now knew the identity of Currer Bell, and Charlotte was much complimented and fêted in London (see 'Life', pp.27–31).

Villette

Summary

Lucy Snowe, a young orphan, has left the relatives with whom she is living to stay with her kindly godmother, Mrs Bretton, who is a widow with a handsome young son, John Graham. The household is soon joined by a relation, a quaint small girl, Paulina (or Polly) Home. When her father joins her, Polly welcomes him with rapture. Graham is intrigued by her oddity, and she becomes fond of him.

Lucy returns to her relatives, and passes the next eight years in an unexplained alternation of tranquillity and turmoil. She describes herself as a young woman already faded, and one who tries to avoid all distress and upheaval. She becomes a companion to the crippled Miss Marchmont, whom she loves, but the old lady suddenly dies.

Without employment, and almost without money, Lucy arrives in London on a bitter night. She weeps desolately, but knows that somehow she will find strength to go forward. She decides to seek work in Belgium, and on the boat her fellow-passengers include a sprightly girl of seventeen, Ginevra Fanshawe, who is returning to her school in the town of Villette. Ginevra tells her that her headmistress, Mme Beck, needs an English assistant, and Lucy takes the coach to Villette. A handsome young Englishman assists her, and she finds herself outside Mme Beck's school. After much scrutiny from M. Paul Emanuel, Mme Beck engages Lucy to look after her three young daughters.

Mme Beck is a widow, and Lucy is impressed by her charm and her control of her school—a control largely exercised through spying. In time Lucy is required to teach English in the school, and although terrified, she subdues her turbulent class.

Ginevra turns out to be a charming, flighty girl with a secret admirer who gives her jewels and clothes. A young English doctor, known as Dr John, comes to attend at the school, and Lucy recognises him as the man who helped her on her arrival. She soon observes that Mme Beck is in love with him.

One summer evening a box containing a love-letter is dropped at Lucy's feet in the garden. Reading the letter and realising the fulsome outpourings cannot be for her, she is interrupted by the arrival of

Dr John, who begs her not to inform Mme Beck. Entering her room one evening, Lucy finds Mme Beck going through her private drawers, but she is more amused than outraged. Soon she sees another letter dropped from a window into the garden. She gives it to Dr John, who is perturbed about the reputation of the charming girl (whose name he does not reveal) to whom it is addressed.

The fiery little M. Paul, who teaches part-time at the school, is producing the school play, and he demands that Lucy takes the part of a foppish young man. He locks her in a dark attic, where she tries to learn her part among rats and cockroaches. During the performance she observes that Ginevra directs her performance at Dr John, and later learns that Ginevra has also another admirer, the elegant Count de Hamal, whom she thinks she will marry because of his wealth and rank. Dr John confides to Lucy his love for Ginevra, and his jealousy of de Hamal.

At the end of the term Lucy successfully conducts her English examinations, to the irritation of M. Paul. Then, left almost entirely alone in the long summer vacation, she becomes lonely and depressed. Feverishly she walks through Villette (Brussels) and the countryside, then one evening enters a Catholic church and on impulse goes into the confessional. The priest is kind, but when she leaves she faints in the street. She regains consciousness in a pretty room, in which she begins to recognise objects and pictures. At last she recognises Mrs Bretton, and realises that Dr John is none other than the boy she knew as Graham Bretton. Her joy is overwhelming, and she begins to recover rapidly. Dr John speaks to her again of Ginevra, whom he believes to be both innocent and beautiful, and Lucy gives vent to her own opinion. He takes her on walks and drives, and she discovers the pleasure of looking at pictures. Alone in a gallery, she encounters the pungent little M. Paul, who teases and bullies her. Reluctantly persuaded into an elegant pink dress, Lucy is taken by the Brettons to a concert. Ginevra is present, with some wealthy friends, and Dr John angrily observes her sneering at his mother, and flirting with de Hamal.

Sadly Lucy leaves the Brettons and returns to her school. She realises she is beginning to love Dr John, and longs for his letters. M. Paul observes her unhappiness, and angers her with his inquisition. With heartless amusement, Ginevra describes to Lucy her cruel treatment of Dr John. Two weeks later M. Paul angrily hands Lucy her longed-for letter, which she hides in her private desk. Later, while she is reading the long, friendly letter, she suddenly sees in the gloom the apparition of a nun. Terrified, she runs to Mme Beck, and in the confusion becomes frantic at losing her letter. However, Dr John, who was on the premises, finds it and returns it, dismissing the 'nun' as nonsense and remarking that she is nervous and unwell.

For the first time, Lucy begins to believe in happiness. When Dr John calls unexpectedly to invite her to the theatre, she is frightened by a light in an alcove in the attic. There is a fire in the theatre, and Dr John assists an injured girl. She and her father are English, and Lucy and Dr John help them home to their fine great house.

For a dreadful seven weeks Lucy does not hear from Dr John. When Mrs Bretton invites her to their house again, Lucy finds there the girl who was injured in the theatre. The girl, who is delicate and pretty, recognises Lucy, and Lucy finally perceives that she is the quaint little Polly, from Bretton, now Paulina May Home de Bassompierre. Lucy observes with pain that she and Dr John are greatly taken up with each other. She now spends most of her free time with the Bassompierres or the Brettons. Miserably, she realises that she will now never receive another letter from Dr John, and she buries her small packet of his letters under a pear-tree in the school garden, realising that she is also burying her lost hopes of love. Once again she encounters the ghostly nun.

Lucy joins her friends at the annual Address given at the principal school in Villette, where M. Paul delivers an impassioned speech on freedom and the future of Europe. At dinner afterwards he is rude to her, but later apologises and offers to take her home. One day Lucy is obliged to interrupt one of his classes, and clumsily breaks his spectacles. To her astonishment, he behaves charmingly, but that evening berates her for her new frivolous clothes.

On M. Paul's birthday everyone except Lucy presents him with flowers. He is so angry with her that he breaks into a furious attack on the English, which Lucy boldly opposes. Later she gives him presents she has made, and is amused at his childlike delight. He wishes to teach her arithmetic, and is pleased when she finds difficulty, but becomes morose as she improves, and she ends by throwing his books on the floor.

Among Mme Beck's friends Lucy sometimes meets a mysterious girl, Mlle Sauveur, who is said to have some connection with M. Paul. Out in the garden, she passes her buried letters, and speaks aloud a painful farewell to Dr John. M. Paul hears her, and as they talk the 'nun' rushes past them. When Lucy visits the Bassompierres after they have returned from abroad, Pauline tells her that Dr John had written to her, declaring his love, and Lucy encourages her to respond.

M. Paul takes the school for a springtime picnic, and asks Lucy what she would feel if he went away for some years. She is greatly upset, and that evening sees him and Mme Beck talking agitatedly in the garden. She realises he is looking for her, but, perversely, she hides from him. She is sent by Mme Beck to deliver fruit to Mme Walravens, and finds herself in a gloomy house in an ancient square. Mme Walravens rudely refuses her gift, and an old priest, who also lives there, reveals himself as the priest to whom she once made confession. He tells her that everyone in the house is supported by M. Paul, who had loved Justine-Marie, the grand-daughter of the malevolent Mme Walravens, who had died long ago. Lucy is much agitated by this adventure. After she is involved in an unpleasant episode with two of M. Paul's superiors, who accuse him of cheating, she lets him know that she has heard his secret history. He begins to avoid her, but she finds pamphlets in her desk commending Roman Catholicism, and M. Paul and the priest take her to Catholic ceremonies, but she will not abandon her Protestant faith.

Dr John and Paulina are eventually married, to live a long and happy life. Lucy feels they are perfectly suited, and reiterates her belief that some are born both fortunate and good, but she knows her own lot is otherwise. Suddenly Mme Beck informs the school that M. Paul is leaving. Lucy's suffering is terrible, and he never comes with an explanation. She angrily condemns Mme Beck's jealous efforts to keep them apart. On Midsummer night—the night scheduled for his departure – she takes a sleeping draught prepared for her by Mme Beck, but its effect is to excite her wildly. Eventually she makes her way to the public park, where there are great crowds for a carnival entertainment. She sees the Brettons and the Bassompierres, as well as Mme Beck and her circle. She has recently gathered from rumours that M. Paul has been pressed by Mme Beck, Mme Walravens, and others of the family, to go to Guadaloupe to retrieve the Walravens estate. Suddenly Lucy hears the name 'Justine-Marie', and the comely young woman she knows as Mlle Sauveur appears with M. Paul. He is now booked on a later boat, and meanwhile cheerfully joins the party and makes much of Mlle Sauveur, evidently his ward. With agonising certainty, Lucy believes that he will marry this girl on his return. Filled with anguish, she reaches her bed at school, only to find it laid out with nun's clothing and a note of farewell addressed to her.

In the morning, Ginevra cannot be found, and Lucy's belief that she has eloped with de Hamal proves correct. Soon Ginevra writes to Lucy explaining how clever Alfred has been in using the disguise of the nun to visit her. At last M. Paul arrives. He is agitated by Lucy's paleness, and as they walk through the town he speaks tenderly to her. He shows her a pretty house, and she finds it is to be her own school. He explains that Mlle Sauveur is merely a ward, and he begs Lucy to wait for his return. She is so full of joy she can even bear his departure.

For three happy years she prospers at her school, sustained by his long letters. When he is on his way back there is a fearful storm in the Atlantic, and many ships are wrecked. The author leaves the end of her story ambiguous, but her meaning appears to be that M. Paul was drowned.

The writing of *Villette*

The novel was probably begun in the autumn of 1851. Charlotte was still suffering acutely from the deaths of her sisters and brother in 1848−9, and she was often ill. For some months early in 1852 she wrote nothing, but she managed to finish the book by November, and it was published in January 1853. For much of the background she made use of her unpublished novel, *The Professor*, but *Villette* is far more than a rewriting of that story.

Plot and structure

The central concern of the plot is to display the development of Lucy, and its chief events are arranged to this end. But although the book is given consistency and direction by Lucy's narration, the plot is frequently halted or interrupted. It is also awkwardly broken into parts; the first chapters are devoted to the Brettons and Polly, with Lucy as a shadowy spectator; the next lengthy section is much concerned with Lucy's feelings for Bretton; only in the last third of the book does Paul Emanuel begin to take a dominating part, and Lucy's life achieve direction and purpose.

The major events emerge from three sets of love-stories; those between Polly and Bretton, Ginevra and de Hamal, and Lucy and M. Paul. Lucy's own story moves along chiefly through her reactions to people or events thrust upon her. Almost against her will, the occurrences of the plot compel her towards growth. As in *Jane Eyre*, vital turning-points in the plot rely on highly improbable coincidences; Lucy's unrecognised cousin Graham happens to be the man who helps her on her arrival in Belgium, happens to be passing when she faints in the street, and happens to find that the girl he rescues from the fire is Polly.

An apparatus of Gothic horror (see 'Writings', pp.32−40), centring on the 'nun', is closely woven into the plot. In part the Gothic is mocked, and shown to be absurd, yet it also has a serious symbolic meaning, in representing the world of illusion and fantasy run wild. The nun's four appearances are closely linked to certain highly emotional moments of Lucy's life. They occur when Lucy cannot find Graham's letter; when she is about to depart with him for the theatre, where he will meet Paulina; when she first talks intimately with M. Paul; and when, after the nightmare of the carnival, she tears the nun's vestments and tramples on them.

The 'double ending' of the story is not very satisfactory. In a letter to her publisher in 1853, Charlotte commented on the alternatives she provides. She called both of them 'fearful', indicating that either death or marriage could have proved equally dire for Lucy. Charlotte's father had requested a happy ending, but the equivocal last paragraphs were the best Charlotte could do for him.

The structure may be awkward, and the plot halting, but the story is nevertheless held firmly together by the consistency of Lucy's view. The force of her inner drama is so intense that it over-rides all structural defects.

Themes

The chief themes are all encompassed within Lucy's story. Through her we see a reconciling of the rational and the passionate, as she grows painfully from an observant shadow, through repression and despair, to a loving, liberated, independent woman.

Lucy's plain face is no accident; Charlotte did not wish to allow her any superficial advantage at all. Although Jane Eyre is also described as plain, she has an elfin charm which is not permitted to Lucy, who must make her own way, without looks or sparkle, on her inner resources only. And Paul Emanuel is as plain a man as Lucy is a woman. This contrast between outward plainness and inward strength (prefigured in the crippled Miss Marchmont) is central to the book, and is neatly reversed in the beautiful, shallow Ginevra and the handsome dandy, de Hamal.

The growth from repression to liberation of emotion is a crucial part of Lucy's development. She begins her adult life as an inhibited young woman, of cold appearance, who learns to break out of the prison of her repression, and welcome love. The writer Harriet Martineau complained of *Villette* that all the female characters think only of love, and it is true that romantic love is central to all Charlotte's novels. She never underestimates its power, for good or for ill, and it forms a large part of Lucy's emotional life. Nevertheless, Harriet Martineau's criticism is not just. Lucy thinks about much else besides love, and one of her concerns, especially towards the end of the book, is the question which haunted Charlotte herself of how it is possible for a woman to reconcile love and marriage with an independent spirit. In all her novels there is an attempt to find an answer to this teasing problem in the master/pupil relationship, and *Villette* is no exception. Lucy willingly places herself under the fierce tutelage of M. Paul, because his tyranny stirred her on and 'gave wings to aspiration'. But once the pupil has learned all the master can teach, what then? Charlotte is no more successful in providing a conclusive answer in *Villette* than in *Shirley*. Lucy established in independence, with a lover far away, enjoys 'the three happiest years of my life', and the reader is left with no certainty that, for her, marriage and independence could have been reconciled.

Just as Shirley warns Louis (Sh) that he would do better to remain a lover rather than become a husband, so perhaps Lucy too found her best solution in those 'three happiest years'.

The opposition of Nature and Art forms a recurring theme in Lucy's growth. Ginevra and de Hamal, she with her devices of allure and he 'so booted and gloved and cravated', are presented as elaborate works of artifice. Lucy and M. Paul, however, are unaffected, uncontrived, and in every way more 'natural'. M. Paul is much associated with the garden, and with the picnic field where he is so happily himself; while storms, the weather, and the imagery of nature are used to reflect the inner turbulence of Lucy's sufferings.

Lucy progresses painfully from a life of fantasy and the experience of books, to reality and experience of her own. At the beginning of her adulthood she knows life only through 'books and my own reason', but as her experience grows greater the importance of books grows less. The picture gallery, Vashti's performance in the theatre, and Lucy's own small venture into acting, are all significant in opening up a real life of feeling and experience. This progress is also expressed through the recurring figure of the nun, and the horror of the carnival. Before Lucy can finally achieve a realistic understanding of the world, the illusion of the nun must be stripped away. So too her drugged perceptions of the carnival, with all its pasteboard trickery, must be finally dispersed in the clear light of day. 'Day-dreams,' she realises, 'are the delusions of the demon'. She still has great pain to undergo, but she has shed her illusions, and she is now strong enough to confront her final tragedy.

Characters

General: Charlotte is always greatly interested in external appearances, and nowhere more so than in *Villette*. The marked unloveliness of Lucy and M. Paul is strongly contrasted with the beauty of Ginevra, Bretton, and Paulina. Most of the characters are based on people she knew, though none are precise portraits; Mme Beck and M. Paul, for instance, are drawn from the Hegers (see 'Life', pp.27-31). Bretton from Charlotte's publisher George Smith, and much of Lucy from Charlotte herself.

Lucy Snowe: As the book is so intimately Lucy's, something of her character has already been considered under 'Themes'. Her personal growth, the problems of marriage and independence, the master/pupil relation, and the surrender of illusion are all mentioned in that section. Lucy is probably the most complex of Charlotte's heroines, and it is clear from Charlotte's letters and observations that she reflects her author in many ways. Charlotte always thought of herself as plain, and Lucy's looking-glass brings her 'a jar of discord'. She protects herself with a cold reserve, and her name is not 'Snowe' for nothing.

She enters the novel as a girl from nowhere, and her long metaphor of shipwreck indicates some family calamity which is never explained. She is 'homeless, anchorless', and in spite of the kindness of the Brettons, very alone. She has little experience of the outside world, and lives vicariously through the lives and writings of others, playing the part of spectator and recorder, 'a mere looker-on at life'.

Her chosen stance as observer includes observation of herself, and a deep interest in her own states of mind. *Villette* is a novel about a writer writing a novel; as Lucy observes and describes others, so, with increasing perception, she observes and describes herself. Her whole story is a voyage of self-discovery.

In spite of her repressed manner, she knows that she is not truly cold. 'Oh! my childhood! I had feelings . . . I *could* feel', she cries. But the unexplained calamity of her childhood left her power of feeling 'in catalepsy and dead trance'. This freezing of emotion has left her inert. She longs for peace, and hopes to achieve it by avoiding all decision and change. With Miss Marchmont 'I would have crawled on . . . for twenty years', and even so early in her life she understands that 'I must be stimulated into action. I must be goaded, driven, stung, forced to energy'. Her burst of enterprise in reaching *Villette* rapidly subsides in Mme Beck's nursery, and again she has to be goaded into becoming a teacher, because she finds herself 'unstirred by impulses of practical ambition.' Her passivity inclines her to remain in one place, but she is forced into action by collision with obstacles. These will not let her be, but demand reactions. Miss Marchmont dies, Mme Beck insists. Above all, she is goaded and shaped by Paul Emanuel. He is hectoring and arrogant, but she gladly accepts his system of 'demands, rejection, exaction and repulse' because it arouses her. His abrasive manner does not cow her, it stirs and inspires. He 'warmed the blood in her veins' and raised not only her ambition but her fighting spirit. It is chiefly he who leads her from books to life, and from illusion to reality; with Bretton, she realises, she was 'likely ever to remain the neutral, passive thing he thought me'. She is convinced she is feeble, but clearly she is not. Under great difficulties and strain, she gets herself to London and Belgium; she is not worsted by Ginevra's cruel teasing; she is perverse enough to withhold M.Paul's birthday present; and when she is offered a position with the Bassompierres, she declares that she is 'no bright lady's shadow'.

The long thaw of her emotions begins when she encounters Bretton and the staff and pupils of the Pensionnat. She falls half in love with Bretton, and discovers for herself the joys and agonies that accompany love; she disapproves of Ginevra, but nevertheless sees her as someone in whom life dances and flows; above all, she is stirred by M. Paul – first to indignation, anger, and amusement, then to jealousy, anguish, and love. She had always longed for affection and love. As a child she had been touched by Polly's trust, later she is overwhelmed by the affection of little Georgette Beck, and after her breakdown she is filled with affectionate gratitude for the kindness of the Brettons. She requires affection in order to feel alive – 'Left alone, I was passive; repulsed, I withdrew'. Her long periods of loneliness undermined her to such a degree that she becomes ill, and even finds herself in a Catholic confessional box. She wishes also for the love of a man, but she wants it on terms of her own. She dislikes the plump sensuality of the Cleopatra portrait in the gallery, she does not approve of Ginevra's obsession with love, and in the end she finds Bretton shallow and vain. She becomes painfully aware that for her at least love is not easy, and both with Bretton and then with M. Paul she suffers the anguish of jealousy and rejection.

Lucy likes to settle for a balanced view, avoiding extremes. When the infuriated M. Paul makes her abandon the Cleopatra portrait in the gallery and sit instead opposite the grim pictures of a woman's life, she finds them 'as bad in their way as . . . the Cleopatra in hers'. This search for balance is also indicated in the contrast between her and M. Paul; she is northern, he is from Spain; she is gentle, he is fiery; she is Protestant, he is Catholic.

When a puzzled Ginevra asks Lucy, 'Who *are* you, Miss Snowe?' Lucy can only reply that she is 'a rising character'. But she also notices that she is seen by different people in different ways. Mme Beck sees her as 'learned and blue', Ginevra as 'ironic and cynical', M. de Bassompierre as 'the pink and pattern of governess correctness'. Perversely, and to Lucy's amazement, M. Paul sees her as something different again – 'too airy and cheery – too volatile and versatile – too flowery and coloury'. These various views hint at the diversity of her personality, and also assist in presenting a portrait more lively and rounded than, as narrator, she could present of herself. It is not until the end of the book, when she has achieved love and independence, that Lucy herself recognises the kind of person she is. She has emerged into a full life of feeling, found her own rich personal experience, and discarded fantasy. She had once valued 'the strange necromantic joys of fancy' but by the end of her story she is prepared 'to penetrate to the real truth'.

For the whole of her life she has indeed been 'a rising character'. She rises from being a repressed, unnoticed child, almost a nonentity, to a mature and balanced woman, filled with a 'genial flame'. She is inert until she is compelled to move, but then she finds she is capable of response, and slowly her rich potential becomes developed and defined.

Paul Emanuel: Charlotte took a great interest in the names of her characters, and it cannot be by accident that M. Paul's name is Emanuel, or 'saviour'. He is in many respects the saviour of Lucy. It seems he is about as ugly as a man could be. He appeared to Lucy as 'a harsh apparition, with his close-shorn, black head, his broad, sallow brow, his thin cheek, his wide and quivering nostril', and Ginevra is not contradicted when she attests that he is 'hideously plain'. He is also very short, and almost always carries the description 'little'. A man further removed from Charlotte's Angrian heroes would be hard to imagine, and the change is very deliberate. In him, as in Lucy, her interest has shifted towards hidden depths of character, and she emphasises this change by demonstrating how goodness may reside in an ugly shell. At first M. Paul's character seems no more attractive than his appearance. In his determination to dominate he is irritable and bullying, and when provoked 'fumed like a bottled storm'. He is suspicious of all superiorities and skills in others, and Lucy soon perceives that he is driven by 'A constant crusade against the "amour-propre" of every human being'. By this means he sustains supremacy, and feeds his love of power. Lucy notices that 'This idea of "keeping down" never left M. Paul's head', and usually she obliges by permitting herself to be kept down. He is deeply suspicious that she knows both Greek and Latin, and is concealing her learning from him. He is a pitiless critic of her clothes, learning, and behaviour, and it is his good fortune that she can endure this treatment and even find it stimulating.

He is irritated by those who fear him, but is immediately gentle when a wrong-doer expresses regret, as Lucy finds when she causes his spectacles to break. He is very sensitive to slights, and sits in a sulky fury when she seems to have no birthday-present for him. His learning and his 'tomes of thought' impress Lucy, and she finds that 'His mind was indeed my library'. At the same time she senses in him not only learning, but an intuitive understanding of life, which she knows she does not possess.

Although he is anti-Protestant and anti-English, she admires his hatred of oppression, and the passion for justice he expresses in his speech at the Athénée. Only towards the end of the story does she realise how great is his kindness to the selfish Mme Walravens and her circle, and how great his generosity in renting and furnishing a house for her school. She realises in the end that he is a 'magnificent-minded, grandhearted, dear, faulty little man', of deep feeling, honour, and piety, whom she prefers 'above all humanity'.

He takes an improbable view of Lucy, far removed from her own or that of anyone else. She is 'too airy and cheery', and she requires 'checking, regulating, and keeping down'. It is he above all who is responsible for creating Lucy, and stimulating her into her full being. His love for her overcomes all obstacles of religion, family, and distance.

M. Paul is based on M. Heger, with whom Charlotte fell in love when she attended the Brussels school (see 'Life', pp.27-31). But although they have much in common in their teaching skills, their fiery temperaments, and their patriotism, M. Paul is not a life-portrait but an engaging, complex character of fiction.

Graham Bretton ('Dr John'): Lucy first meets Graham when he is a young man and she is still a child. He grows up tall, handsome, and kind. Although they do not recognise each other, he helps Lucy when she arrives in Belgium, and again six months later when she faints in the town. His affection is marked as she recovers at his house, but he does not notice she is falling in love with him, and his few letters thereafter are merely friendly. He is in love with the beautiful, flighty Ginevra, and only when he observes her sneering at his mother at the concert does he realise her shallowness. He is popular as the doctor at the Pensionnat, and especially popular with Mme Beck, who is greatly attracted by him and jealous of his friendship with Lucy.

He has fine qualities, and it is with unbearable sadness that Lucy realises that he is turning his attention to Paulina. But she begins to recognise his failings, and thinks at the theatre that he is 'impressionable' but 'unimpressible'. He is vain, requires the world's approval, and looks for 'the adjuncts that Fashion decrees, Wealth purchases, and Taste adjusts'. In Paulina he finds all he wishes, and Lucy sees how perfectly they are matched. Bretton and de Hamal (together with St John Rivers in *Jane Eyre*) share the godlike Greek beauty of which Charlotte seems to have been always suspicious.

Paulina Home (de Bassompierre): She first appears as an articulate, precocious, enigmatic child, one of Charlotte's most intriguing portraits of children. She grows into a woman who is beautiful, kind, quiet, concerned for Lucy's feelings, and delicate in describing her own. She is thoughtful and well-read, and in comparison with Ginevra 'shone pre-eminent for attractions more subtle and spiritual'. Yet Lucy can never quite take her seriously. She and her father seem never wholly to grow up, and Lucy is sometimes relieved to escape their doting companionship. When she thinks of Paulina she is reminded of M. Paul's silky little dog. Paulina, like Graham, is someone on whom fortune always shines; 'Some lives are thus blessed,' writes Lucy. '. . . it is the attesting trace and lingering evidence of Eden.'

Ginevra Fanshawe: She is of 'light, careless temperament and fair, fragile style of beauty'. A vivacious, worldly girl, she is not of wealthy family but she cultivates fashionable friends, and is impressed that de Hamal is both a colonel and a count. She thinks of little but 'conquests' and marriage, and is delighted with Dr John's attentions, although she finds him too serious. She flaunts his devotion before the suffering Lucy, and is piqued when he falls in love with Paulina. The air of secret intrigue surrounding the 'nun' disguise greatly delights her. Although at school she is interested only in music and dancing, she is shrewd, and it is she who asks the penetrating question, 'Who *are* you, Miss Snowe?' Lucy intrigues her, and though she teases her cruelly, she seeks Lucy's company and asks her opinion. Lucy thinks of her as a person with 'an entire incapacity to endure. They seem to sour in adversity, like small beer in thunder'. But in this Lucy was wrong. After her elopement, Ginevra survives great financial problems. Her self-absorbed letters leave Lucy with the conviction that Ginevra will always prevail, because she is incapable of suffering, and fights 'the battle of life by proxy'.

Madame Beck: She is an enigmatic character, of greater significance than the space she occupies in the book. The atmosphere she creates in her Pensionnat is both friendly and malevolent, open and eerie, and she lurks balefully in the background of Lucy's life. She is pleasant, plump, and comely, and her system is to please all, parents and pupils alike. The school is efficiently organised, and liberal in its curriculum and attitudes, while Mme Beck smiles inscrutably and remains apparently calm. She enjoys worldly pleasures, and spends many evenings at concerts, plays and balls, when her school imagines she is asleep. But all is not what it seems. The efficiency of her system is based on continual spying and eavesdropping, as she glides about in her 'shoes of silence'. She spies on Lucy in the school and in the garden, and she finds and reads Dr John's letters. Her soft-footed haunting of the school contributes greatly to the atmosphere of mystery created by the 'nun'.

She is greatly attracted by Dr John, and begins to make herself 'complete as a model, and fresh as a flower'. She is jealous of Lucy's letters, and becomes spiteful when she realises that Lucy and M. Paul are beginning to love each other. She is a relative and ally of the sinister Mme Walravens, and is one of those who put pressure on M. Paul to go to Guadaloupe. Lucy sums her up as 'wise, firm, faithless; secret, crafty, passionless'.

Miss Marchmont: Although she accounts for only a brief episode in Lucy's life, she made an abiding impression on the girl. 'She gave me,'

Lucy wrote, 'the originality of her character to study, the steadiness of her virtues . . . the power of her passions to admire; the truth of her feelings to trust'. She also gave affection and an occupation, and Lucy had hoped she might 'crawl on' with her for many years, secluded from the harsh world. Miss Marchmont parallels Lucy and M. Paul in exhibiting goodness and courage within an unattractive body, and she also foreshadows much that is to befall Lucy. When Lucy observes of her that 'A vein of reason ever ran through her passion; she was logical even when fierce' she is foretelling her own development; when Miss Marchmont describes her past love and its loss, her story also anticipates Lucy's; the storm and the Banshee wailing foreshadow the storm in which M. Paul is drowned. Miss Marchmont's benign influence appears again at the end of the story, when the money she leaves Lucy pays for the extension of the school.

The narration

Lucy is not Charlotte's self-portrait, but there are marked similarities, and much of Lucy's development, and much of her experience, parallel Charlotte's own. Charlotte, like Lucy, lost her mother when she was very young; she had been both teacher and governess; and she had been for two years at the Hegers' school in Brussels, where she had fallen in love with M. Heger. Like Lucy, she was plain, clever, and repressed, yet turbulent within. Lucy's growth towards a balance between passion and reason, illusion and reality, parallel Charlotte's inner struggle to throw off the spell of Angrian romance.

After her attempt at objective narration in *Shirley*, Charlotte returned to writing in the first person. The method seems to have come readily to her, and gave her the opportunity to express feelings and attitudes based on her own experience. By her convincing use of the first person, she gives the story a unity of vision reminiscent of *Jane Eyre* and almost entirely lacking in *Shirley*. Although her experience appears so immediate, it is actually being described many years later, when Lucy is a white-haired old lady who has at last found strength and calm—a device also used (and more fully exploited) in *Jane Eyre*.

Style

For the most part the writing is controlled, varied, and precise. The vocabulary is rich, but used with economy. Very little is overblown or bombastic, for in this book Charlotte determined to keep herself 'guiltless of that curse, an overheated and discursive imagination'. Long, controlled sentences are skilfully varied with short, as in the last paragraph of the story: 'Mme Beck prospered all the days of her life; so did

Père Silas; Mme Walravens fulfilled her ninetieth year before she died. Farewell.' The longer sentences are often elegantly balanced, as in Lucy's reflection on herself, beginning 'I seemed to hold two lives' (Chapter 7). Especially in the last quarter of the book, there is a poetic fusion of matter and manner which drives the story on to its vivid, powerful end.

Metaphor and imagery are as animated and effective as anywhere in Charlotte's writing. Sometimes the metaphor is much extended, as when Lucy hints at the mystery of her childhood, beginning 'Picture me then . . . ' (Chapter 4). Sometimes, but rarely, it is overextended, as in the description of Jael (Chapter 12). Metaphor is often used for brief, vivid description; on Mme Beck, 'not the death on Calvary could have wrung from her eyes one tear'; or M. Paul's 'blueness and fire of glance'. Images are often incisive, as in the lines on M. Paul describing 'the low stature, the wiry make, the angles, the darkness' and in the alliterating 'strength of sturdy independence in the stringing of his sinews'. Charlotte enjoys alliteration and uses it for varied effect, including irony, as when the 'nun' turns out to be only a 'buxom and blooming . . . bourgeois belle'. Adjectives are aptly chosen, and verbs often vigorous—as in 'I must be goaded, driven, stung, forced to energy'.

Charlotte's liking for personification is given less scope in this novel, but it remains a favourite device, and one with which the reader of today is ill at ease. When Lucy is hoping for letters from Bretton her feelings are not made any more intense by her reflections on 'divine Hope' and 'Reason'. There are fewer direct addresses to the reader than in the previous novels. The use of French stands out a little awkwardly, and fails to impart the air of authenticity it is intended to convey.

The reception of *Villette*

This drew the best reviews of any of Charlotte's novels, but they were by no means consistently good. The book was held to be coarse and vulgar (though less so than *Jane Eyre*), and Lucy's independent mind was severely reprimanded in the *Christian Remembrancer* (an old enemy). In a letter of March 1853, the critic Matthew Arnold (1822-88) described the novel as 'hideous, undelightful, convulsed' and full of 'hunger, rebellion, and rage'. G.H. Lewes, however, with his usual perception, saw it as a work 'of astonishing power and passion'. It was 'healthful as a mountain breeze' and 'visibly springs from the independent originality of a strong mind nurtured in solitude'. The novelist George Eliot (1819-80) found 'something almost preternatural in its power'.

The poems

Charlotte wrote more than half all her poems before she was twenty. In 1836 she sent some early poems to the poet Robert Southey, but he was not enthusiastic. Many of these early poems were part of the Angrian saga, and their chief subject is Nature. They show great facility, but the language is mostly that of eighteenth-century verse, and the rhythms are over-regular. The poems that she selected for her share in *Poems by Currer, Ellis, and Acton Bell* (1846) include the terrifying 'Gilbert' and some intense dramatic monologues, but only the poems contributed by Emily received any critical attention. Charlotte's most effective poetic writing is found in her novels, when at her best she fuses emotion with image in an intensity more often found in poetry than prose.

PLATE 4: Emily, by Branwell; fragment of an oil painting.

Part 3

Emily Brontë

Her life (1818–1848)

Born in 1818, Emily was two when her father moved his family to the parsonage at Haworth, and it remained her home and her haven for the rest of her life. Apart from a year with Charlotte in Brussels (1842), and some brief local visits in the north, her times away were always unhappy and she longed to return to the parsonage and the moors (see 'Home and family' pp.11–13). When she was three her mother died, and the children's Aunt Branwell looked after them until her death in 1842.

In 1824 Emily was sent to join Charlotte at the Clergy Daughters' School at Cowan Bridge, where her older sisters, Maria and Elizabeth, were already boarders. It was a harsh, unhappy place, and Emily was miserable and ill. She and her sisters were all brought home at various times in 1825, and soon both Maria and Elizabeth died of tuberculosis, either contracted at the school or made worse by the conditions there. At home the four surviving children were taught a wide range of subjects by their father, and Emily eventually taught herself French and German. She became an accomplished pianist, and (like all her family) a talented sketcher. The girls were taught needlework by Aunt Branwell (though they learned reluctantly), and Emily in particular became skilled in the kitchen. She loved to encourage their old servant, Tabby, to talk of the days before the coming of the mills, and she would take over the family cooking if Tabby was ill. Mrs Gaskell, in her *Life of Charlotte Brontë* (1857), describes how Emily would stand in the kitchen kneading the dough for bread, with her book of German grammar propped up in front of her. But Emily's greatest passions were for writing, and for the moors.

The moors begin at the back door of the parsonage, and all her life Emily loved to walk great distances across them, either with company or alone, or with her mastiff, Keeper. She loved the moors in all seasons and weathers, knew the remote and secret corners, and made herself familiar with their birds, animals, and flowers. She would bring wounded creatures home, including once a hawk she called Hero, and tend them in the outbuildings at the back of the parsonage. Fear and danger seem not to have bothered her. She pummelled her mastiff's eyes to make him obedient, and once cauterised her own arm with hot metal when she had been bitten by a mad dog. This incident is the basis of an episode in *Shirley*, and Shirley herself is to some degree a portrait of Emily.

Charlotte's friend Ellen Nussey described Emily as lithe and active, the tallest of the family (although they were all small), but also the shyest, reluctant to speak to anyone outside her family circle. Of all the Brontës, Emily is the most elusive, and the most intriguing.

Charlotte and Branwell gave their younger sisters parts in the Glass Town saga (see 'Unpublished writings, pp.23–6), but by 1831 Emily and Anne were beginning to break away, to create their own vast epic of Gondal. Emily wrote her Gondal poems and stories in a minute printed script, which was not deciphered until the 1920s. Gondal never lost its hold on her, even when she was writing *Wuthering Heights*, and the loss of the entire work except for the poems (and some other writings entirely separate) is one of the great misfortunes of literature. But even in early youth she did not write only of Gondal. She wrote other poems, and she scribbled her occasional 'diary-papers', filled with exuberant, exclamatory detail and giving the most intimate account we possess of the Brontës' daily lives.

In 1835 Emily was sent as a pupil to Roe Head, where Charlotte was a teacher, but she became so ill and wretched that after three months she was brought home for good. There she continued her education, on her own and with her father, and wrote on obsessively, through the labyrinths of the Gondal story. She was also secretly writing poetry, some interspersed in the Gondal saga, and some independent of it. In 1837 she felt she should seek independence, and relieve some of the burden on her father, and she took a teaching post at Law Hill School, near Halifax. There she had time for walking, riding, and writing, but (according to Mrs Gaskell) she could not endure it for more than six months, and once again came home. Branwell was also home again, having given up his studio in Bradford. Charlotte and Anne were beginning to lose patience with his drinking, but Emily still staunchly defended him.

1840 was a happy year for Emily. Anne was also at home again, and their days were much enlivened by the presence of their father's new curate, the charming and witty William Weightman, with whom, it seems, Anne fell in love. In 1841 the sisters devised a plan to start a school in the parsonage, and Emily and Charlotte accepted with gratitude when Aunt Branwell offered them financial help to improve their languages by studying in Brussels. Early in 1842 they left for the Pensionnat Heger, where Emily's French and German, as well as her essays, music, and drawing, received the highest praise.

Learning of Aunt Branwell's death at the end of the year, she and Charlotte returned to Haworth, and Emily remained at home, taking up her old home life, returning to Gondal and her poetry. While Anne and Branwell were teaching the Robinson children at Thorp Green, Emily was at home with her father, who taught her pistol-shooting in the garden. When Charlotte returned from Brussels at the beginning of 1844, the sisters published their prospectus for a school, but there was no response. In the same year Emily divided her poems into two sections, the 'Gondal' and the 'Philosophical' and copied them out, neatly and legibly, in separate books. She was writing some of her most accomplished poetry about this time, and Gondal was still a vital part of her creative life. It was probably in this year that Emily started work on *Wuthering Heights*. When Charlotte came upon some of her poems Emily was angry, but eventually agreed to Charlotte's plan to have them published, with a selection of Anne's and her own. *The Poems of Currer, Ellis and Acton Bell* (Charlotte, Emily, and Anne) were published in 1846. The masculine-sounding names were chosen in the hope that the poems might be taken seriously, but only two copies were sold. One reviewer, however, singled out the 'inspiration' of Emily's work.

Two months after the publication of the poems, the sisters sent off their new manuscripts; *The Professor*, by Charlotte; *Wuthering Heights*, by Emily; and *Agnes Grey*, by Anne. They did not find a publisher until the summer of 1847, when T.C.Newby accepted the novels of Emily and Anne (provided each contributed fifty pounds), but rejected Charlotte's. No effort was made to publish until after the success of Charlotte's *Jane Eyre* in the autumn, but both novels appeared in December. A few perceptive reviewers commended the power and originality of *Wuthering Heights*, but it was almost universally condemned, often in the strongest terms, as crude, unpleasant, and even diabolical. Although it began to sell, Emily did not live to see any truly appreciative public comment

It seems that she was soon engaged on another book. When she was very ill, towards the end of 1848, Charlotte wrote to Newby on the subject of a second work by 'Ellis', and later declared, in her 'Biographical Notice' to the edition of 1850, that even after the poor reviews of their first books, Emily and Anne were 'prepared to try again'. However, it soon became clear that Emily had advanced tuberculosis. She refused to see a doctor, and she died in December in the sitting-room of the parsonage.

Writings

All that remains of Emily's work is *Wuthering Heights*, and just under two hundred poems. The long saga of Gondal, in which many of the poems were embedded, has disappeared; and her project for a second novel, which she was considering in 1848, was cut off by her death.

She seems to have been happy only at home at Haworth, and in the inner world of her imagination. The domesticity of the kitchen and parlour within, and the wild spaces of the moors without, seem to have given her all she needed to develop as a writer. As a child she was as precocious as the rest of her family, and her early writings were a vital part of her growth as an author (see 'Unpublished writings, pp.23–6). Gondal took as powerful a hold on her imagination as Angria took on Charlotte's. Emily and Anne were still developing Gondal stories and acting Gondal roles as late as 1845. Charlotte found the break from the high-flown romance of Angria painful and difficult, but Emily's poems and novel seem to grow directly from the soil of Gondal. Many of the poems were a part of the Gondal story, and the drama of *Wuthering Heights*, centred on the twin triangles of Heathcliff, Cathy and Edgar in the one generation, and Hareton, Catherine and Linton in the next, have their root in the Gondal entanglements of Augusta, Julius and Aspin. With its two islands, warm and cold, and its embattled, contrasting characters, Gondal seems to have become for Emily not only an absorbing story but a symbol of the human mind.

Together with the rest of her family, Emily was wide open to the literary influences of her day. The Gothic novels of Horace Walpole and Mrs Radcliffe, and their followers, were deliberately vague and ambiguous in style. So too, the longer Romantic poems of Lord Byron, and much of the work of Sir Walter Scott, dealt in dramatic, cloudy emotions designed to move the reader by their scale rather than their depth. Emily devoured these works. They held her imagination and influenced her deeply, both in her poetry and in her prose. The noble, tragic figure of the 'Byronic hero' lends much of his wild glamour to Heathcliff.

Emily, however, was no imitator. When she came to write herself she was not thrown off balance by Gothic romance, nor was her writing in any way affected by its overblown rhetoric. While preserving the intensity of feeling, and some of the violence of action, she rejected their cloudy concepts for a vivid, concrete imagery all her own. Her skill in expressing high emotion in precise symbol and image is shown throughout her poetry and prose, and it is that which makes *Wuthering Heights* so poetic a novel.

The open freedom of the moors seems to have been essential to her happiness and her creativity. As Charlotte wrote in her Memoir to the editions of 1850, 'Liberty was the breath of Emily's nostrils; without it, she perished'. The themes of liberty and repression, dungeons and freedom, recur constantly in the poetry. For her the rugged northern landscape had a moral and emotional significance far beyond everyday concerns. She never uses the world of nature for mere decoration, nor is it often examined minutely; it is invoked chiefly in its grander aspects, to intensify emotion and illuminate meaning. It pervades all her writing, and provides the dominating theme which binds her work. In both poetry and prose she draws most of her imagery from nature. Rocks and trees, weather, wild animals, fire and water are repeatedly drawn upon, and contribute greatly to her individual style. Her use of varied and vigorous verbs, which take the sentences striding on, and give force to the verse, also contribute much to her distinctive voice.

Her longing to be free of the body and at one with the forces of nature runs through her poetry, and recurs repeatedly as a theme in *Wuthering Heights*. This impulse towards the impersonal and the general is characteristic of Emily, and alien to Charlotte. Although Emily's characters live their lives in a recognisable everyday world, they also take on a significance which suggests that they are not only themselves but representatives of eternal truths. Eternity is very real to Emily, both in the life of the earth and in the after-life of man. Like Heathcliff and Cathy, she seeks in her poetry a union with 'infinite immensity'. Access to the world of spirit comes easily and naturally to her, and is expressed in both her poetry and prose; after her death, Catherine Earnshaw (Linton) haunts Heathcliff and haunts the rest of the book. Dreams, too, provide Emily with a rich quarry of symbols, and an entry to the mysterious world beyond prosaic everyday life.

In writing of her sister in the 1850 edition of *Wuthering Heights*, Charlotte said, 'I have never seen her parallel in anything. Stronger than a man, simpler than a child, her nature stood alone...'. Even allowing for Charlotte's sisterly prejudice, there is truth in what she says. Emily's forceful, creative originality is felt on every page she published.

Wuthering Heights

Summary

The events related in the story begin in the mid-1770s and continue until 1802. The actual telling of the story, by Lockwood and Nelly Dean, covers only the years 1801-2. Emily uses the name 'Cathy' for both Catherine Earnshaw and Catherine Linton; this summary will follow the usual custom of using Cathy for the mother, and Catherine for the daughter.

In 1801 Mr Lockwood describes in his journal how he rented Thrushcross Grange, a handsome house set in a park in a Yorkshire valley. He goes up to Wuthering Heights, a fine, neglected farmhouse on the moors, to visit his landlord, Heathcliff. Although Heathcliff has a gentlemanly look, he and his old servant, Joseph, are grimly unwelcoming. When Lockwood returns the next day he meets an un-couth young man, Hareton, and a wild-looking young woman. Heath-cliff tells him that his wife and son are dead, and the young woman is his son's widow, Catherine. Snow is falling, and when he wishes to leave he is ignored. The dogs knock him down, and the housekeeper, Zillah, shows him to a bed for the night.

In his enclosed box-bed Lockwood sees a series of names – Catherine Earnshaw, Catherine Heathcliff, Catherine Linton – scratched on the sill, and finds some old books written over in a child's hand, twenty-five years before. He dreams, then wakes to find a branch tapping the window; in his next dream he breaks the window to catch the branch, only to find his hand grasping small, cold fingers, as a voice sobs to be let in, crying that its name is Catherine Linton. He sees a child's face, and in his terror cuts the child's wrist on the broken glass of the win-dow. The voice moans that it has been a waif for twenty years. Lock-wood's cries bring Heathcliff, to whom he relates his dream, and he later hears Heathcliff crying out for Cathy to return.

(In the next chapter the double narration begins, with Lockwood telling the reader what Ellen Dean tells him.) Ellen Dean, acting as Lockwood's housekeeper at the Grange, explains the complex family relationships. The young woman at the Heights is Catherine, the daughter of Edgar Linton and his wife Catherine (or Cathy) Earnshaw. This daughter had married her cousin, Linton Heathcliff, now dead, and is also cousin to Hareton, the uncouth young man at the Heights. Mrs Dean, who had long ago been nurse and companion to Cathy and her brother Hindley, up at the Heights, describes how their father, old Mr Earnshaw, had once brought home a swarthy urchin from Liver-pool, whom he named Heathcliff. He and Cathy had become devoted as children, but Hindley hated him. Eventually Hindley was sent off to college. When old Earnshaw dies, Hindley returns for the funeral with a wife, Frances. Hindley, now master at the Heights, banishes Ellen, Cathy and Heathcliff from the living-room, and Heathcliff is made to work as a labourer on the farm.

One night Heathcliff returns alone, and tells Ellen how he and Cathy had been secretly gazing through the windows of Thrushcross Grange at the Linton children, Edgar and Isabella. But a dog bit Cathy, mak-ing her faint, and she was taken into the house.

After five weeks Cathy returns to the Heights transformed into a young lady, and jeers at Heathcliff's boorish manners. When the Lintons come to dinner Heathcliff cannot contain his jealousy, and pours hot sauce over Edgar. Hindley beats him and locks him in the attic, where Heathcliff, filled with hatred, begins to think of revenge.

Ellen's story then moves on to the next year, the summer of 1778. A son, Hareton, is born to Hindley and Frances, but Frances dies soon after. Distraught, Hindley begins to drink and gamble, and oppresses Heathcliff until he becomes yet more savage and unkempt. Although Edgar Linton has fallen in love with Cathy, he dares not come to the Heights for fear of Heathcliff. Cathy asks him to call when no-one is there, and eventually they confess their love for each other. Later, not realising Heathcliff is hidden in the shadows, Cathy tells Ellen that she has agreed to marry Edgar, because Heathcliff has become too brutalised to be marriageable. At this point Heathcliff creeps away, too soon to hear Cathy describe how she feels her soul to be at one with his, and how she would not be separated from him even after marriage. She rushes out to find him, into a moorland storm, and returns drenched; but Heathcliff does not come back, and she becomes feverish. Edgar's mother brings her down to the Grange, where the old people both catch the fever and die. Cathy, however, recovers, and three years after Heathcliff's disappearance she marries Edgar. Ellen describes their happiness, even though it is based on his fear of her.

Some six weeks after their wedding, Heathcliff appears at the Grange. He is now clean and well-dressed and very handsome, and Cathy is so delighted to see him she greatly distresses Edgar. Heathcliff is living with Hindley at the Heights, because Hindley wants a companion in his drinking and gambling. Edgar's sister, Isabella, is delighted with the new Heathcliff, and when she falls in love with him, Heathcliff sees an opportunity to forward his revenge on the Lintons. When Cathy discovers him embracing Isabella she is enraged. He protests that Cathy has behaved cruelly to him, and soon Edgar and Heathcliff come to blows. Heathcliff escapes, and Cathy determines that if she cannot have them both she will break their hearts by breaking her own. She locks herself up, and refuses to eat. She becomes ill, and in her delirium imagines herself to be with Heathcliff up at the Heights.

The doctor reveals that Isabella has run away with Heathcliff, and angrily Edgar rejects his sister. Heathcliff and Isabella are away for two months, and Cathy recovers from the worst of her illness. Ellen then receives a letter from Isabella, describing her return to Wuthering Heights after her marriage; Hindley fears he may kill Heathcliff, to whom he has now lost most of his money; and Heathcliff locks his bedroom against her, so she is forced to sleep in the filthy sitting-room.

Heathcliff, handsome and spruce, insists he must see Cathy, and eventually persuades Ellen to help him to visit the Grange. When he enters Cathy's room he seizes her in his arms. She claims that he will forget her when she dies, but he cries that he could as soon forget himself. He accuses her of betraying their long love, and Cathy replies that if she was at fault she is now dying for it. As they weep together, Edgar returns from church to find Cathy in Heathcliff's arms. That night, in giving birth to a daughter, Cathy dies. Ellen finds Heathcliff out in the night, distracted with grief, and calling on Cathy's spirit to haunt him.

On the day after Cathy's funeral, Isabella rushes into the Grange, bleeding from a wound under the ear. She tells Ellen how she had taunted Heathcliff with Cathy's death. He had thrown a knife at her and she had thrown it back, then fled. Ellen then relates how Isabella travelled south, where she gave birth to their son, Linton, a pale, sickly child. When the infant Catherine is six months old, Hindley dies, and because of Hindley's debts to him Heathcliff becomes the owner of the Heights, where he treats Hareton like a slave.

In the course of the next twelve years, Catherine grows into a lively, beautiful child, who is never allowed to wander beyond the confines of the Grange. But when her father leaves to visit Isabella in the south, Catherine becomes inquisitive and restless, and escapes up to Wuthering Heights. She has heard nothing of her cousin, Hareton, who is handsome but illiterate and uncouth. When Isabella dies, Edgar brings her son, Linton Heathcliff, home with him, and Catherine is disappointed to find him frail and querulous. Heathcliff then demands that his son should come to live at the Heights.

Linton remembers nothing of his father, who jeers at him for his fair skin and frail body. But Heathcliff assures Ellen he will look after Linton, because the boy must one day inherit the Grange as well as the Heights. Catherine does not see Linton for four years, until one day she and Ellen encounter Heathcliff on the moors. He persuades them to come to the Heights, explaining that he wishes Catherine to marry Linton one day. He tells Ellen that he has revenged himself on Hindley by brutalising Hareton, who is an illiterate laughing-stock to Catherine and Linton. Edgar forbids Catherine to see Linton again, but Ellen discovers that they are writing love-letters to each other.

Edgar falls ill, and Ellen tells Catherine not to cause him concern over Linton. One day when Catherine is accidentally locked out of the park, Heathcliff rides by and tells her that Linton is dying for love of her. Reluctantly, Ellen goes with Catherine to the Heights, where Linton is full of complaints, and begins to cough so violently that Catherine has to spend all morning soothing him. She is told she must not see him again, but when Ellen is ill she meets Linton every evening. Ellen catches Catherine returning from the Heights, and Catherine tells her that when she had jeered at Hareton he had turned her and Linton out of the room, and Linton had coughed blood. Hareton later said he was sorry, but she cut at him with her riding-whip. Catherine is again forbidden to visit the Heights.

Ellen tells Lockwood that all this happened just a year ago. Edgar felt that he was dying, and invited Linton to the Grange; he now wished the cousins to marry so that the Grange should be Catherine's when he died. When Catherine and Ellen go to see Linton they find him exhausted on the moor, hinting at a secret. Heathcliff compels Catherine and Ellen to help him to bring Linton back to the Heights, where he locks them all in. When he is out of the room, Linton explains that his father insists that he and Catherine marry at once. Heathcliff warns Catherine that if she does not marry Linton immediately she will be kept prisoner until after her father's death, and he locks her and Ellen in an attic. In the morning he takes Catherine away.

When Ellen is let out after five days, Linton is married to Catherine, and boasting that her inheritance is now his. Edgar is at the point of death, but he despatches servants to rescue Catherine, and tells Ellen that he wishes to alter his will, to protect Catherine's inheritance. But the lawyer has already been bribed by Heathcliff, and will not come. Catherine escapes in the night, in time to see her father before he dies. Heathcliff now demands that Catherine live up at the Heights. He tells Ellen how he had prised away the side of Cathy's coffin, and told the sexton that his own should be opened in the same way, so that their bodies would crumble together.

Coming to the end of her story, Ellen tells Lockwood she has not been allowed to see Catherine. Linton had received no medical aid, and Catherine was alone with him when he died. Heathcliff showed Ellen Linton's will, leaving all his and Catherine's possessions to him. After spending two weeks alone in her room at the Heights, Catherine came downstairs, and found Hareton. She refused to read to him, and he swore at her. Ellen can relate no more of the story, and Lockwood says he intends to give up his tenancy of the Grange.

Lockwood then describes how he went to Wuthering Heights, and found Catherine jeering at Hareton's attempts to read. In a rage, he hit her and threw her books on the fire. Resuming his journal later in 1802, Lockwood describes his recent visit to the Grange in September, just before the end of his tenancy. He walks up to the Heights, where Ellen is now living, and there watches through a window as Catherine affectionately teaches Hareton to read. Ellen tells him that Heathcliff is dead. Soon after Lockwood had left the Grange, she had been summoned to the Heights. Catherine and Hareton were on uneasy terms, but growing closer. Heathcliff grew violent when Joseph pointed out the growing affection between the pair. But when he looked at Catherine he saw her mother in her, and could not strike her. He told Ellen he was longing for death which would unite him with Cathy. Although they were in his power, he no longer wished to destroy the Lintons and the Earnshaws.

Heathcliff almost ceased to eat, and became inhumanly haggard. He talked to empty air, and imagined himself with Cathy. One morning Ellen saw the window of his room was open in the rain, and she found him dead in bed, smiling, and with a grazed wrist. Some of the villagers and Joseph asserted they had seen the spirits of Heathcliff and Cathy on the moor. Hareton is greatly distressed by Heathcliff's death, but he and Cathy are to be married at the New Year. As they return from a walk, Lockwood quietly leaves.

The writing of *Wuthering Heights*

Emily probably began the novel in 1845, after the failure of the sisters' plan to open a school, but she was secretive about her writing and the date cannot be certain. She had completed the book by July 1846, when it was first sent to a publisher, together with Charlotte's *The Professor* and Anne's *Agnes Grey*. It was not accepted until June 1847, and she had to contribute fifty pounds towards the cost. The publisher, T.C. Newby, was in no hurry to publish until the success of Charlotte's *Jane Eyre* spurred him on, in the hope that 'Ellis Bell' would profit by the reputation of 'Currer Bell'. The novel appeared in December 1847.

Plot and structure

The plot centres on the lives of two generations of two families, one living starkly up on the moors at Wuthering Heights, and the other comfortably in the valley at Thrushcross Grange. The dreadful events which haunt both families arise primarily from Cathy's wrong-headed decision to abandon Heathcliff and marry Edgar Linton. For many readers the dark presence of Heathcliff dominates the story, and it is indeed chiefly he who links the lives of the two generations. He attempts to twist their destinies, and he almost destroys them, but his thirst for revenge dies before he has completed the destruction. Hareton and Catherine survive to bring the story to a tranquil end.

At first reading, the narrative may appear confusing. Although it is narrated by Lockwood and Ellen Dean in the course of the years 1801-2, the events it relates begin in the mid-1770s, and are told in retrospect. Emily does not supply many dates, and indeed it was not until 1921 that C.P. Sanger revealed the details of the elegantly structured plot, and the consistency of dates and times within it. The details of the moors and the valley round Gimmerton are equally consistent and precise, and the elaborate process of law by which Heathcliff intended to join the estates of the Earnshaws and the Lintons are accurately recorded. This precision of detail is an aspect of the book which is easily overlooked in the grandeur of the conception. Emily is never blown off course by the tempestuous passions which rock the lives of her characters. Because of her firm attachment to facts, she was able to keep under control the hectic excess of the Gothic romances (see 'Life', pp.93–5) which so stimulated her imagination. In the same way, Ellen's recital of past events provides a distancing in time, which gives perspective to the turbulent events of the story, removing the raw immediacy which might have strained their credibility.

For all the rich complexities of the book, the plot is simple and symmetrical. Hindley Earnshaw and his sister Catherine live at the Heights, Edgar Linton and his sister Isabella live at the Grange. Catherine Earnshaw (referred to hereafter as 'Cathy') marries Edgar Linton, and has a daughter, Catherine; Hindley marries, and has a son, Hareton. This symmetry is violently disrupted by Heathcliff, the foundling, who loves Cathy, then marries Isabella and has a son, Linton. The lives of the three children of the second generation (Hareton, Catherine, and Linton), are equally disrupted by Heathcliff, but after Catherine's brief forced marriage to her cousin, Linton, she marries her other cousin, Hareton. In the first generation Cathy Earnshaw becomes Cathy Linton; in the second, Catherine Linton becomes Catherine Earnshaw. Rough Earnshaw energy is again fused with civilised Linton calm, and on this second attempt harmony is at last established. Some readers feel that the second half of the book, after Cathy's death, loses some of its driving force. Yet the re-establishment of the family relationships in the second generation, the gradual elimination of the baleful influence of Heathcliff, and the slow movement towards peace and hope is as moving, in its gentler way, as the tempests of the earlier story.

The unity of such a complex novel is achieved in various ways. It would be difficult to find an episode, or even a detail, which could be described as irrelevant. Everything has its point, everything has significance in contributing to the story. Emily's use of names, although at first confusing, is very deliberate, and helps to hold the book together. Catherine Earnshaw's daughter is also called Catherine in order to bind the generations, and to demonstrate how the wrong decisions of one generation redound upon another. It also serves to emphasise the renewal of the family triangle (Catherine, Hareton, Linton) in the second generation. Heathcliff's son has as his Christian name the surname of the Lintons, so emphasising his disastrous Heathcliff-Linton blood. Heathcliff himself was given only the one name, pointing to his isolation as a boy from nowhere. The dominance of 'H' names – Hindley, Heathcliff, Hareton – emphasises the connection with the Heights, and also means that the lovers of the second generation, Hareton and Catherine, replicate the initials of Heathcliff and Cathy. The name and date on the lintel of the Heights, 'Hareton Earnshaw 1500', establishes the great age of the farm and its long line of Earnshaws. The names of the houses echo the nature of their inhabitants; 'Wuthering', the name given to the barbaric Heights, is a local word meaning 'atmospheric tumult', while Thrushcross Grange, with its gentle Linton owners, carries a suggestion of thrushes, linnets, and the Christian connotations of 'cross'. Lockwood, too, is a significant name, suggesting that this effete and shallow man has shut off the dark places he does not understand.

The gripping, bewildering opening of the first four chapters establishes, with astonishing economy, the domestic situation at the Heights in 1801, where a savage Heathcliff bullies Hareton and Catherine. It conveys Heathcliff's obsessive passion for Cathy, and tantalises the reader with her old diary, her three scribbled surnames, and Lockwood's dreams; and it introduces the two narrators, the tenant, Lockwood, and the housekeeper, Ellen Dean.

Narration

The elaborate structure of the narration is an integral part of the book, which could well have failed without it. The author hides herself behind two narrators, both of whom have distinct characters of their own. The chief witness of events is the competent, prosaic Ellen Dean, but her narration is contained within Lockwood's. She had grown up at the Heights, as the nurse and companion of Hindley and Cathy Earnshaw, then had moved down to the Grange as housekeeper when Cathy married Edgar Linton. She has an intimate knowledge of both houses and both families, and of the country in which they live, and she forms a vital link between both places, as she is inextricably bound to both families. Her details of the daily life within the two houses give a solid credibility to the background, and it is largely through her sterling but limited mind that the tumultuous events of the story are filtered. Her solid nature acts as a breakwater, protecting the reader from scenes so violent, and so cruel, that without her they might seem mere melodrama. She has clear likes and dislikes; she is often irritated by Cathy, and she is contemptuous of Hindley's wife, Frances. But she is never overwhelmed by her encounters with violence or passion or death, and in this way she steadies the turmoil. However, the situation is yet more subtle. The careful reader begins to realise that Ellen's judgement is not always reliable. She is not a mere sounding-board, but a human being who sometimes makes mistakes. She was wrong in her complacent assumption that Cathy and Edgar were deeply happy, and wrong in attributing Hindley's decline to Heathcliff's hatred. And she is never quite able to comprehend the scale of the emotions and events around her.

The book opens and closes with passages of direct narration by Lockwood. The reader may pity poor Lockwood for his first experience of Wuthering Heights. He is soaked, frozen, kicked, snubbed, seated on some dead rabbits, set upon by dogs, and terrified by dreams and visions. Any humour the book possesses may be found in Lockwood's first knockabout confrontation with his landlord, Heathcliff.

The first and obvious reason for Lockwood's existence in the novel is that Nelly needs an audience for her story. But beyond this is the author's wish to cushion the incredulous southern reader against the harsh realities of northern life. Lockwood is a southerner, unused to northern ways and northern weather. His vain, conventional nature comprehends little of the passionate lives into which he accidentally intrudes, but at least he has the virtue of curiosity, and urges Ellen on with her story.

Lockwood and Ellen are both subtly employed to enlist the reader's sympathy for the awkward Cathy. The stilted, superior tones of Lockwood's journal contrast sharply with the simplicity of Cathy's, and Nelly's exasperated 'She's fainted or dead . . . so much the better' provokes sympathy for Cathy's hysterical outburst.

These are the two direct narrators, but clearly neither could have been present during all the events of the story. The narration is therefore supplemented by Nelly's reporting of episodes described by other witnesses, such as Heathcliff, Isabella, Cathy, Catherine, and Zillah.

Lockwood and Ellen provide, as it were, two windows through which the reader peers into the story. Other 'windows' are provided by the various characters whose accounts Ellen quotes. Indeed, the 'window' image pervades the book, both as a metaphor and as an actual physical sheet of glass (see 'Themes', below).

The narration is constructed in such a way that there is rapid transition from one episode to the next, with no long linking passages in which tension might drop. Although the period of the story covers some twenty-five years, the narrative does not proceed in smooth chronological order. There are several deliberate dislocations of time, in order to emphasise certain events: Ellen begins her story to Lockwood twenty-five years in the past; Lockwood reads the diary written when Cathy was twelve, but Ellen's story later returns to Cathy when she was younger still. The evening of Heathcliff's and Cathy's first visit to the Grange, Cathy's death, and Heathcliff's death, are all presented out of their strict chronological order, in order to emphasise their significance.

Themes

The novel is conceived on so ambitious a scale that much of what it 'means' must lie on the borders of the communicable. The roots of its power lie deep, and on this level it may be seen as a map of the human mind, in which Heathcliff and the Heights represent the dark, elemental forces, and the Lintons and the Grange the virtues of civilisation. It can be seen also as Emily's exploration of her own self, mapping the division of her being between the wild, untamed moors and the domesticity of the hearth at home. From this deep division, displayed chiefly in the antagonism between Heathcliff and Edgar, the story moves slowly, through great trouble and pain, towards the final marriage of these two elements in the marriage of Hareton and Catherine, a coming together of the Heights and the Grange. Cathy, in her worldly choice of Edgar, senses the impossibility of marriage with Heathcliff, who is 'herself' – both are children of the Heights. In marrying into the Grange, she is groping towards something she has not yet known, but her identity with Heathcliff and the Heights is so strong she cannot bridge the chasm. It is only in the second generation that her daughter Catherine and her nephew Hareton achieve a harmony between the warring elements. This power of generalisation, of carrying her characters beyond the point where they are merely individuals, gives a universal significance to Emily's work. The story is not only about the inhabitants of two houses, it is about human nature.

Heathcliff is the disordering cause which creates disaster in two families. In his wake, he carries passion, hate, jealousy, and revenge. Without him Cathy's marriage would no doubt have proceeded calmly enough, and nothing would have changed at the Heights or the Grange. But as Heathcliff injects violence, so also he brings energy; the turmoil he causes in both families is in the end a new source of strength for the second generation. Emily deliberately demonstrates Heathcliff's brutality, and Cathy's childish wilfulness, yet it is difficult not to feel that her own sympathies were weighted in favour of the Heights. Her imagination is more passionately engaged by those who belong to the moors than by those in the valley, or even by those who in the end combine the two. This is not to say that she rejects the need to harmonise the wild and the tame, the fierce and the gentle; but her own personal love for the wild and untamable led her deepest sympathies in that direction.

The members of the two families are shown, not only in their relations to each other, but in a relationship with the world of nature. Heathcliff in particular is described in terms of rocks and trees and wild animals. The weather, both storm and shine, constantly reinforces mood and event; when Cathy decides to marry Edgar, a violent storm shakes the Heights; Hareton, in whom hope for the future resides, is born on a summer morning in haytime; when Lockwood makes his final visit to the Heights, and tranquillity is restored, he sees 'the mild glory of a rising moon'. This constant association of man and earth emphasises still further the universal nature of Emily's vision. The earth abides, in rock and water and cloud, and man is bound to it. There is also a hint, in the experience of Heathcliff and Cathy, that the spirit survives the grave, not in a conventional Christian sense, but as a part of the earth to which it belongs. The theme of escape from the body into Cathy's 'glorious world' runs through her life and Heathcliff's, as it runs through Emily's poems (see 'The poems', pp.117–21). Cathy's vision is of freedom beyond the grave, and Heathcliff's is of union with her there.

The final resolution of the story may be seen as the end of a long history of sin and expiation. Cathy's betrayal of Heathcliff, which he cannot forgive, creates a ramifying series of disasters, and is visited on the second generation. This betrayal is not expiated until, after great suffering to both families, Hareton and Catherine finally come together in love.

Love is the most obvious and immediate theme of the novel. It is explored in many aspects, ranging from the obsessive passion of Heathcliff, through Hindley's joy and desolation, Lockwood's feeble fancies, Isabella's infatuation, and Edgar's gentle devotion, to the slowly built, strongly based love of Hareton and Catherine. Heathcliff and Cathy often speak of each other in semi-religious terms, as if their love were on some unworldly plane, both deeper and more spiritual than the loves of others; Heathcliff calls her his 'soul', and she feels that he offers a reality far beyond her own. But Emily does not elevate this high romantic passion beyond the quieter and more domestic loves of Edgar, Hareton or Catherine. Although it is more magnificent in scale, it is also shown to be more destructive and unforgiving.

The use of 'windows', both real and metaphorical, was mentioned under 'Narration' (pp.104–5 above). There are many examples throughout the book of this insistence on the image of windows; the child's wrist dragged over the broken window glass is the first occasion when someone 'outside' wishes to be let 'in'; later Heathcliff and Cathy gaze through the window of the Grange, spellbound by the warmth and luxury within; later still, Cathy insists that the window be opened, when she wishes to die; and when Catherine and Hareton finally come together, the excluded Lockwood watches them through a window.

The novel's persistent element of savagery, even of sadism, is closely involved with the Heights. The theme is established early, with Lockwood's description of drawing the child's wrist over the broken glass; later Heathcliff hangs Isabella's pet dog, Hareton hangs a litter of pups, Linton tortures cats for his amusement. Stabbing and cutting images are frequent; Isabella shrieks as if pierced with 'red-hot needles', and cold weather cuts Nelly 'keen as a knife'. On a number of occasions small children are threatened with death; old Mr Linton thinks the boy Heathcliff should be hanged, the infant Hareton is threatened with murder by his drunken father, Heathcliff wishes the law would permit him to vivisect Linton and Catherine.

Belief in superstition and the supernatural is rife at the Heights. Joseph is frightened by Catherine's threat to make a wax model of him, and he believes she has bewitched Hareton. Nelly wonders if the young Heathcliff may be a ghoul or a vampire, and fears he may haunt her; Cathy and Heathcliff believe the churchyard is haunted, and indeed a belief in ghosts is commonplace. Heathcliff's belief that he is haunted by Cathy's spirit is both joy and torment to him, and Joseph and the villagers believe they see the ghosts of Cathy and Heathcliff together on the moors.

Style

The staple prose of the book is straightforward, bold, and spare. Except for the great speeches, such as Cathy's beginning 'I cannot express it' (Chapter 9), which rise to a passionate poetic strength, the writing is unemotional and restrained, as if deliberately curbing the tumult it describes. The transitions from one event to another are done with economy and pace, in lines such as 'One step brought us into the family sitting-room' or 'That Friday made the last of our fine days'. Detail is vivid enough to bring a scene to life, but it is not overloaded.

Emily's frankness of expression brought her much abuse. She did not shirk the honest description of events, and she shocked even her sisters with her particularity; Heathcliff's violent embrace of Cathy when he returns, and the strangled dog with 'pendant lips streaming with bloody slaver' are only two of many passages which provoked outrage.

One of the sources of Emily's strength is her use of imagery, and in this her prose often approaches the condensation of poetry. Her images are largely drawn from the natural world, and most of them from the harsh expanses of the moor. On her first page, Wuthering Heights is presented as a grim, wind-blown place, where the limbs of the twisted thorn-trees make man and nature one in the kind of image which recurs throughout the book. People are constantly described in metaphors of landscape and the elements; Edgar differs from Heathcliff 'as a moon-beam from lightning', Cathy is struck by 'a tempest of passion'. Wild animals are much used in descriptions of Heathcliff, who is 'a wolfish man', an 'evil beast', and 'foams like a mad dog'. The moors provide descriptions of him as 'furze and whinstone', and his own speech is filled with images of wind and trees. Fire and water are also frequent sources of imagery; the fire in the hearth is always a potent symbol of comfort for Emily, but fire is also much used as the source for verbs of branding, kindling, and flashing; and water for gushing, boiling, steaming, and heaving. Gentle animals are often referred to with contempt; Edgar is 'a sucking leveret', Linton is 'a puling chicken', Hareton 'a calf'. But not all frail things are despised.

Catherine is 'soft and mild as a dove', and at the end of the book moths flutter over Heathcliff's grave, and a soft wind blows through the grass.

This vigorous use of specific imagery gives each scene a life which is almost visible and audible; Lockwood hears 'a chatter of tongues' and 'a clatter of culinary utensils', and sees the light and heat in the pewter dishes. The language is condensed, often with the economy of poetry. Cathy's simile of the wine shows a poet's skill in concentration; her dreams, she says, have 'gone through and through me, like wine through water, and altered the colour of my mind'. The energy of the verbs, often employed as metaphors, urges the sentences on. Even inanimate objects are often given verbs of motion, as when the kitchen is 'forced to retreat', abuse is 'lavished', illness is 'weathered'.

Emily moves easily and naturally among symbols (see also 'Themes', pp.105-8). The symbols at the heart of the book are of wild and tame, fierce and gentle, dark and fair. But there are also innumerable lesser symbolic acts and events. On the night Heathcliff rushes away in despair, a storm splits a great tree, representing his rupture with Cathy; his hair and hers are wound together in a locket; Lockwood's closet-bed is like a coffin, and in it Heathcliff eventually dies. Hareton's flower-garden, which so enrages Joseph, is a touching symbol of his wish to please Catherine, and to establish something beautiful at the Heights.

Characters

Heathcliff: Although Heathcliff is created entirely in Emily's terms, aspects of his character, and the events of his life, have some possible historical sources. When Emily taught at Law Hill in 1837-8 she must have heard the story of its builder, Jack Sharp, who was, like Heathcliff, an adopted orphan, who took over the estate on which he was brought up, and ruined a member of his adopted family through gambling. She would also have heard a story of her father's, about an ancestor of his who found a dark, dirty boy in a ship and adopted him. Through his cunning the boy eventually took over the family estate, and degraded the young heir, Hugh, who was Emily's grandfather. The story of the Cumbrian, Richard Sutton (1782-1851), has recently been revealed as yet another possible source. Sutton was a young foundling, adopted and brought up in Dentdale, who rose to dominate his adopted family and their estates.

However, the character of Heathcliff, as distinct from his circumstances, owes most to the life and poetry of Lord Byron. In Thomas Moore's (1779-1852) biography of the poet, Emily would have read of Byron's childhood deprivations and resentments, his fascination with rebellion and crime, his cruelty to his wife, and his thwarted passions. In Byron's poetry she would have encountered heroes of mysterious origin, who rebelled against authority, felt themselves to be alone and apart, and fell passionately in love. Like many of these heroes, Heathcliff is dark, handsome, and magnetic; he realises that Isabella sees him as 'a hero of romance'. But he is also uncouth and cruel. In this demonic aspect he is reminiscent of John Milton's (1608-74) Satan, whose high possibilities were blighted by impossible ambition; the child Heathcliff is as dark as if he 'came from the Devil'.

On the simplest level, Heathcliff stands as a figure of violent energy, in opposition to the effete refinement of the Lintons. He has been described as representing 'the principle of storm', standing for an indestructible force which outdistances the petty concerns of everyday. In Cathy's words, he is 'a wilderness of furze and whinstone, winter and wolves', and throughout the story he is identified with rock and storm and wild things. When in her dream Cathy is flung onto the moors, she wakes sobbing for joy because she is with Heathcliff, and Heathcliff is the moor. His name alone demonstrates his affinity with moor and rock. At a deeper, mystical level, he 'is' Cathy; when she cries 'Nelly, I *am* Heathcliff', and declares he is always in her mind 'as my own being', she is speaking of an identity so deep that Heathcliff must be seen as representing a part of her own soul. He is a recognisable human being, but he is also a cosmic force, and it is from this aspect of his nature that his resonant power arises. His mysterious origins as a foundling also hint at some aspect that is not merely human. Nelly wonders if 'the little dark thing' is a fiend, or a vampire; Cathy refers to him as a Satan; and Isabella asks if he is a devil.

His driving longing to be body and spirit with Cathy, alive or dead, is a consequence of the psychic identity between them; one cannot be whole without the other. After her death, he is obsessed with her image, with his suffering, and with his longing to have her back. His desire for revenge on the Earnshaws and Lintons swells to a sadistic excess. He becomes savage against a world which has taken her from him, first by marriage and then by death, and his destructive hatred develops as a revenge against Cathy herself, in a desire to hurt and destroy all she loved. 'I have no pity!' he cries, and he has none. He begins to exult in causing pain, and broods on torture; he longs to vivisect Catherine and Linton, and to crush the entrails of the 'worms' who surround him. He so terrorises Isabella that she flees; he encourages Hindley's degradation through drink and gambling, and possibly murders him; he cheats his way into obtaining the Grange, brutalises Hareton, terrifies his son into signing over the Heights, and forces his marriage with Catherine. Only towards the end does he find his efforts turning to ashes; 'I have lost the faculty of enjoying their destruction,' he cries. Something at last has touched his heart; he feels some twisted affection for the loving Hareton, and he sees Cathy's eyes in Catherine.

He has moments of understanding, as when he perceives the roots of Isabella's infatuation in romance, but in general his absorption in himself and Cathy is so devouring that other people exist only as objects of hatred and revenge. Throughout he sees himself as the injured victim, and perceives the entire tragedy as Cathy's responsibility. 'I have not broken your heart,' he says to her, 'you have broken it; and in breaking it, you have broken mine.'

After Cathy's death he soon loses all his early attraction. Between that time and the moment when he at last rests beside her, 'my cheek frozen against hers', his dignity disintegrates. He becomes slovenly and morose, sustained only by his vengeance and his obsessive desires. Even in death he is frightening, with a 'frightful life-like gaze of exultation', and sharp white teeth between parted lips.

Heathcliff is created on a grand, elemental scale, but he is not a tragic or a heroic figure. As a child, he was wild but not wicked, and Nelly found his desire to please Cathy very touching. But he neither recognises, nor struggles against, the madness of his obsession. Although he may be greatly pitied, his creator in the end rejects him in favour of a more harmonious and less selfish love. Emily's fervent imagination was probably more deeply engaged by him than by any other character in her story, but she was not deceived by his Byronic splendour. Just as she restrained the excesses of her plot with precise and prosaic detail, so she saw through the flamboyance of her hero, and saw to it that he devoured himself.

Catherine Earnshaw/Linton: For most of her brief life Cathy is a compelling and attractive character, with whom her creator seems deeply engaged. She is a wayward, high-spirited girl, full of mischief – in Ellen's words 'a wild, wicked slip' – and her affections are strong. When her brother Hindley inherited the Heights, she and Heathcliff were left much alone together, and often they roamed all day on the moors. Her childhood spent outdoors with him was the time of her most brilliant happiness. Out there in the wild she felt her profound affinity with Heathcliff and with the untamed earth; the moors were 'heaven itself'. When she declares that Heathcliff is as necessary to her as 'the eternal rocks beneath' she is acknowledging that he is a part of her very nature. With stumbling perception, she tries to express this conviction more than once; she feels she cannot marry him 'because he is more myself than I am' and 'as my own being'. On her side the relationship seems barely sexual or romantic at all, but something even more fundamental; she cannot see how her marriage to Edgar could affect it. She tells Nelly that she *is* Heathcliff, that separation from him is impossible, that 'Whatever our souls are made of, his and mine are the same'. She believes 'If all else perished, and *he* remained, I should still continue to be; and, if all else remained, and he were annihilated, the Universe would then be a mighty stranger'.

Heathcliff is the heart of her strength, and when he leaves she begins to lose control. She slaps Nelly, shakes Hareton, and strikes Edgar. She cannot endure pain, weeps constantly, and is filled with self-pity. When Heathcliff returns she feels herself an angel filled with radiance; but his marriage to Isabella, and the violent antagonism between him and Edgar, finally unhinges her.

The worldly part of her feels that by marrying Edgar she can actually help Heathcliff. This naive immaturity runs all through her relation with him. She cannot comprehend that he has grown to be a man, that childhood is over, and that their joyful childish companionship has grown, for him, into a devouring adult passion. Her own feelings seem to be almost asexual. Even though she embraces him on his return, her identity with him, and her profound need of him, are lacking the sexual feelings which move him so strongly.

In spite of her distaste for the uncouth young Heathcliff, Cathy knows she should never have married Edgar. Ever since her stay at the Grange, after she was bitten by the dog, she had felt the temptation of wealth, prestige, and luxury. Even before her marriage takes place, she can say to Nelly, 'I've no more business to marry Edgar Linton than I have to be in heaven'. Yet she does not blame herself; her immaturity makes it impossible for her to accept responsibility or guilt. She will not fully admit that she has wronged or ill-treated Heathcliff, and she cries, 'I am in no way blameable in this matter'. Heathcliff's accusation of 'infernal selfishness' provokes only outrage. The strain of her situation after Heathcliff's return leads to her increasing derangement. Like a petulant child, she declares, 'If I cannot keep Heathcliff for my friend – if Edgar will be mean and jealous – I'll try to break their hearts by breaking my own.' In her success lies the waste and pity of the first half of the story.

Cathy's cruelty to Edgar is that of a fierce spirit confronted by one that is gentle. She feels for him the same contempt that Heathcliff, in another context, describes to Nelly; 'It's odd what a savage feeling I have to anything that seems afraid of me' and 'The more the worms writhe, the more I yearn to crush out their entrails'. She joins Heathcliff in taunting Edgar as 'a sucking leveret', and urges him to flog her husband 'sick'. Her understanding of Heathcliff's pleasure in inflicting pain arises from her own pleasure in doing the same. In spite of her absorption in him, she finds delight in tormenting him; eighteen years after her death, describing her refusal to appear to him in spirit, Heathcliff says, 'She showed herself, as she often was in life, a devil to me'. Her jealousy of Isabella forces Cathy into recognising the detestable aspects of Heathcliff. She begins to see him as 'an arid wilderness', uncultivated, pitiless, and 'quite capable of marrying . . . fortune and expectations'. The last comment is cruelly ironic, for this is precisely what she herself had done.

Cathy's tragedy lies in the fact that she cannot grow up. In her illness she cries, 'I wish I were a girl again', and when she is confronted with frustration and pain she behaves as a child. She cannot accept the facts of adult sexuality and jealousy, she will not take responsibility or blame, she cannot endure the crossing of her wishes. Her only solution is to break down, dashing her head on the furniture, and grinding her teeth in 'senseless, wicked rages'. She comes to believe that everyone hates her, her dreams and fantasies terrify her, and she cries out, 'Oh Nelly, the room is haunted!'

Nelly Dean, limited in many ways, understands much about her young mistress. It is she and not Cathy who sees why Cathy accepts Edgar. She presents Cathy without romance, and even seems to dislike her. Cathy's fervent lyrical passage on her identity with Heathcliff is met with 'I was out of patience with her folly!'

Cathy and Heathcliff together: The bond between them is of almost mystical intensity, life-long, and unbroken by parting, marriage, or death. Both are obsessed, but both love in different ways. Cathy seems to love Heathcliff as a natural force, and as a part of her inner self, rather than as an individual lover and man; whereas Heathcliff loves Cathy with all the power of an obsessive adult passion. She fails to understand his jealousy of Edgar, and he cannot understand her obtuseness. Their beings are so centred on each other that no-one else is of any account except as an obstruction. Their own lives, and the lives of those around them, are laid waste by their headstrong actions. Even when Cathy is dying, they cannot bring themselves to the reconciliation which might have given both their spirits rest. He cannot forgive her betrayal in marrying Edgar, and she cannot accept her guilt. They can only lacerate each other, pitching Cathy into her final disintegration, and Heathcliff into his twenty years of hell without her. Both long for the release of death, he so that his body and spirit may be blended with hers, she to escape to freedom in 'that glorious world'.

Edgar Linton: In stark contrast with Heathcliff, Edgar represents the qualities of quiet, civilised, comfortable life. In the early part of the book, dominated by the rigorous life of the Heights, he seems a pale, effete creature – in Nelly's words, 'a soft thing'. Heathcliff's contempt does not grow solely from his jealousy; Edgar has the kind of softness which always arouses his desire to hurt. He scorns him as 'a lamb' not worth knocking down, and declares 'he couldn't love as much in eighty years as I could in a day'.

Edgar, however, grows in strength and stature. After Heathcliff's first departure, he treats Cathy with gentle generosity and indulges her whims, nursing her attentively when she is ill, both before and after their marriage. Until Heathcliff's return, it seems that Cathy is happy enough with him, but from the moment Heathcliff arrives great demands are made on Edgar. To most of them he rises generously, but he receives little thanks from either Heathcliff or his wife, and finds himself brushed aside as 'a puling creature'.

But like his sister Isabella, he has spirit; he protests at Cathy's wild joy over the return of Heathcliff, and when provoked altogether too far he strikes Heathcliff a great blow. But his strength is shown less in physical prowess than in dignity, forbearance, and courage. His detestation of Heathcliff makes him hard towards Isabella, but he welcomes their sickly son, and is reluctant to abandon him to Heathcliff at the Heights. In spite of the pain she has brought him, he is devastated by Cathy's death, and apart from visiting her grave he becomes almost a recluse at the Grange. He longs to be reunited with her in death, and when he is dying says, 'I am going to her'. Nelly thought him kind and honourable, and preferred him to Cathy.

Isabella Linton/Heathcliff: Heathcliff first expresses his contempt for her when he and Cathy, as children, see her and Edgar through the window of the Grange. When he returns after his three years' absence, she becomes infatuated with him, attracted by his spruce new look. Even when he hangs her little dog, she does not take warning. As he himself claims, he never shows her any 'deceitful softness', but he is ready to forward his revenge on the Lintons by marrying her for her money, and for the pain her marriage will cause to her family. She elopes with him, but when they return to the Heights she is unable to bear his savagery any longer, attacks him, and flees to the Grange with a knife-cut on her neck. Edgar cannot forgive her for her marriage, and she leaves for London, where Linton is born, and where she later dies.

Hareton Earnshaw: As a baby he was adored by his father Hindley, but after his mother's death he lives in mortal danger from his father's drunken rages. He grows up dark and handsome, but he is neglected and morose. As Hindley declines, Heathcliff deliberately brutalises the boy as part of his revenge, until Hareton 'takes a pride in his brutishness'. After his father's death, Heathcliff forces him to work as a labourer on the farm, and tries to prevent him learning to read or write. He oppresses Hareton as Hindley once oppressed him, and he takes the more pleasure in his cruel practices because he knows Hareton to be intelligent and feeling. He determines that one crooked tree should grow as crooked as the other 'with the same wind to twist it'.

Some part of Hareton, however, resists this corruption. As Nelly perceives, he harbours 'good things . . . amid a wilderness of weeds', and he quietly refuses to remain where Heathcliff wants him, in 'his bathos of coarseness and ignorance'. Just as Heathcliff, as a boy, wished sometimes to be clean and decent for Cathy, so Hareton also washes when Catherine visits the Heights, and is as jealous of Linton as Heathcliff once was of Edgar. He earnestly wishes to better himself, and makes touching efforts to learn to read, in order to impress Catherine. Nor is he discouraged by her scorn, although he can become angry enough to swear at her and throw her books on the fire.

Gradually it becomes clear that Hareton's nature is fundamentally affectionate and forgiving. In spite of the treatment he has received, he loves Heathcliff, and he is the only person to suffer when Heathcliff dies; in Nelly's words, he 'bemoaned him with that strong grief which springs naturally from a generous heart, though it be tough as tempered steel'.

He comes to love Catherine deeply, with a normal adult love far from the tormented passion of Heathcliff. Just as Catherine is a more balanced and gentle woman than her mother, so Hareton is a mirror of what Heathcliff might have been, had the chances of his life been different. At the end of the story Heathcliff comes to regard Hareton as 'the ghost of my immortal love, of my wild endeavours to hold my right, my degradation, my pride, my happiness, my anguish'.

In a moving and symbolic brief scene, Hareton infuriates Joseph by digging up currant-bushes to plant flowers for Catherine. But he and she will not live at the Heights when they marry. They will move down to the kindly Grange, and leave that desolate place to Joseph, and the spirits of Heathcliff and Cathy.

Catherine Linton: From her birth Catherine combines the qualities of the Lintons and the Earnshaws, 'with the Earnshaws' handsome dark eyes, but the Linton's fair skin . . . and yellow curling hair'. It is her destiny to join the two houses in marriage, as well as in her features. Her ideal of happiness is not (as was her mother's) to be dropped on the wilds of the moors, but to rock in a rustling tree, with birds and woods and water all about her, sparkling and dancing 'in a glorious jubilee', with the moors (significantly) in the distance.

She is beautiful and 'gentle as a dove', but she is also bold and high-spirited, without the wilful petulance of her mother. Nelly finds her affectionate and delightful as a child, but when she is twelve her curiosity impels her to disobey her father and ride to the Heights. She becomes much intrigued by her cousin Linton, writes to him secretly, and makes many forbidden visits to see him. She pities him, and treats him gently, but she is openly contemptuous of her other cousin, Hareton, and capable of striking out at him with a whip.

She refuses to be frightened of Heathcliff, who attacks her when she accuses him of having stolen her land, and she contrives to escape from his captivity to see her dying father. After Linton's death, Heathcliff makes her work in the house and destroys her books, but Hareton persuades her not to protest. Imperceptibly her feeling for Hareton grows; she begins to help him with his reading, and eventually discovers that she loves him. When they marry they will restore tranquillity to the two troubled families. They will live down at the Grange, but they will bring their Earnshaw energy with them.

Linton Heathcliff: The ailing Linton represents the gentle qualities of the Lintons carried to effete and enervating lengths. He demonstrates the impossibility of union between Heathcliff and the Lintons. His mother brings him up in the south, but she dies when he is twelve, and he is compelled to join his father at the Heights. He is a pale, feeble youth, despised and resented by Hareton. His nature is petulant and vicious, and he enjoys torturing small animals. His terror of his father is such that he will do anything to avoid his displeasure; his only independent act is to assist Cathy to escape from her imprisonment when her father is dying. He submits to acting as a decoy to lure Cathy and Ellen to the Heights, and to their imprisonment there, and he acquiesces in all his father's plans for his marriage and inheritance.

However, he is not without perception. He is astute about his own failings and deficiencies, as he reveals in the lines to Catherine, beginning 'I *am* worthless, and bad in temper' (Chapter 24). He notices kindness and love, but realises that he is unable to achieve them himself.

Hindley Earnshaw: Like his sister Cathy, Hindley is a creature of extremes. As a boy he is jealous of his father's love for Heathcliff, and he hates and bullies the boy, just as in later years Heathcliff is to hate and bully him. He is sent to college and returns with a wife, Frances, whom he adores, and he is at first devoted to their infant, Hareton. When Frances dies of tuberculosis he is distraught, and his mourning takes the form of cursing God and turning to drinking and gambling. He almost kills the baby Hareton by dropping him over the stairs, and he frequently threatens murder, to Heathcliff and others, but when Heathcliff returns to the Heights he is glad of a gambling companion. When he begins to lose heavily he realises he must keep Heathcliff with him, in the hope of winning back his terrible losses. But Heathcliff acquires a mortgage on the Heights, and on Hindley's death inherits the farm. Joseph hints strongly that after a terrible fight, during which Hindley tried to murder Heathcliff, Heathcliff assisted his opponent to his death.

Joseph: He is an old, leathery, 'vinegar-faced' farm hand, who has been with the Earnshaws many years. His unpleasant character is based on the fanatical Calvinism all the Brontës abhorred. He is wholly lacking in love or charity, gives affection or kindness to none, and takes pleasure in the march to hell of everyone around him. He relishes Heathcliff's brutality to Hareton, because he believes Heathcliff will be damned for it. He is also deeply superstitious; spirits and ghosts are familiar to him, he is terrified when Catherine threatens to make a wax image of him, and he believes she has bewitched Hareton. After Heathcliff's death, he sees him with Cathy on the moor.

Ellen Dean: She is fully described under 'Narration' (pp.104–5).

Lockwood: The temporary tenant in 1801-2 of the Grange, and the narrator of the story. Lockwood too, is described under 'Narration' (pp.104–5).

The reception of the novel

The book was received with almost universal disgust. It was held to be brutal, diabolical, wicked and coarse, and the life it described 'almost savage'. The influential *Quarterly Review* held it to be 'odiously and abominably pagan'. Emily was distressed, and sadly did not live to see the reviews in the *Palladium* and *The Leader* in 1850. The latter, by the perceptive G.H. Lewes, found it 'sombre, rude, brutal, yet true'. He praised the 'vigorous delineation of character' and saw in Heathcliff 'devil though he be...a sort of dusky splendour'. The book, he thought, 'shows more genius . . . than you'll find in a thousand novels'.

The poems

Commentary

Most of Emily's surviving poetry was written during about 1835-45, before she began work on *Wuthering Heights*, and much of it was originally embedded in the lost prose saga of Gondal. Just under two hundred poems survive, which Emily divided in 1844 into 'Philosophical' poems and 'Gondal' poems, all copied out in a tiny but legible hand.

In about 1832 Anne wrote out a list of Gondal place-names and characters, and this has proved invaluable in reconstructing the lost story and in linking the poems. But certain themes and references will probably always remain obscure. The fact that a poem seems very personal does not necessarily mean that it was written outside the Gondal story: the lament 'Cold in the Earth', which seems to reflect an intimate personal experience, is actually spoken by Rosina over the grave of Julius. At the same time, many of the poems, whether part of Gondal or not, probably contain the personal feelings and experience of their author. The problem is to assess what is personal to Emily, and what related only to the characters in the saga.

Themes

A passion for the world of nature runs as an abiding theme through all Emily's work, both poetry and prose. Moorland skies and spaces, dells and copses and rocks, wind, weather, and seasons, dominate her imagery and stimulate many of her profoundest experiences. In 'Shall Earth no more inspire thee,' the dreamer is urged to return, and be satisfied with the beauty of the world. The last verse of 'Stanzas' concentrates the passion for nature which pervades her work:

What have these lonely mountains worth revealing?
More glory and more grief than I can tell:
The earth that wakes *one* human heart to feeling
Can centre both the worlds of Heaven and Hell.

Many of the poems are sad, mournful, or even tragic. Emily was much drawn to themes of suffering, especially of exile, loss, and the struggle towards freedom. As Charlotte wrote, 'Liberty was the breath of Emily's nostrils', and the loss of it is mourned in poem after poem: 'In dungeons dark' and 'The Prisoner', among others, are filled with bitter images of confinement. Despair and loss, often in prison settings, haunt the later poems, in which the captive laments some past joy of childhood, love, or home; 'The Weary Task', filled with the longing for home, is one of the simplest and most personal expressions of this recurring theme. The strife so often expressed between light and dark, the fierce and the gentle, is at the heart of the poem 'Stars', with its images of brilliant, destructive day and the longing for 'Gentle Night'.

Thoughts of death stirred Emily's imagination deeply. Among many other poems, 'Cold in the Earth' and 'The Outcast Mother's Song' imagine death as it affects both the dead, and those left behind. But there is another kind of 'death' which occupies Emily's attention in poem after poem. This is not the death of the body, but the loss of the conscious individual self. She sees the desire for physical death as 'this coward cry', and in 'Self-Interrogation' acknowledges that 'the countless links are strong/That bind us to our clay'; but the loss of personal identity, in a blending with the mystical and eternal life of nature, is a continual longing.

Infinity and immortality are not usually couched in Christian terms: her beliefs owe more to the pantheistic philosophy of Wordsworth and Percy Bysshe Shelley (1792-1822). The 'Strange Powers' for which she waits in 'The Visionary' represent a mystic rather than a Christian force. The 'God' of her poetic vision is not a biblical or a domestic presence, but an image of boundless life, unfettered by creeds. This release from the prison of the self, into a mystical amplitude, appears most simply in 'I'm happiest when most away', a poem in which the poet becomes a 'spirit wandering wide/Through infinite immensity'. It is powerfully expressed, too, in 'The Philosopher', and most splendidly of all in the four lines from 'The Prisoner' beginning 'He comes with western winds'. The return to the reality of the conscious world is seen as an agony, expressed most vividly in 'Ah, why because the dazzling sun', and in the lines in 'The Visionary' in which the mystic cries, 'Oh dreadful is the check – intense the agony/When the ear begins to hear and the eye begins to see'. This last line, lamenting the moment when the flesh again begins 'to feel the chain' links with the multiplying imagery of fetters and prisons in the rest of the poetry.

In her feelings about nature, childhood, and the proper language of poetry, Emily had much in common with Wordsworth, and she knew his work well. Several of her poems, such as 'The Prisoner', convey the same kind of mystical experience as Wordsworth describes in 'Tintern Abbey' and 'The Prelude'. Her 'Stanzas' follows the same line of thought as 'Get up, get up, and quit your books'. Shelley too, is thought to have inspired much of Emily's thinking; 'No coward soul' shares much with 'Adonais' in seeking the spirit at one with eternal nature.

Perhaps the most celebrated (and probably the last) of the poems is 'No coward soul is mine'. This again affirms a faith in a God who is infinity and eternity, but its emphasis on courage is also characteristic. Courage is a quality much praised in the poems; 'The Prisoner' does not give way to 'desolate despair', 'The Old Stoic' prays only for 'a chainless soul/With courage to endure', and the mystic, returning from the ecstasy of his vision, must learn to endure mortality. Courage is also demanded of those who must learn to live without joy; the mourner in 'Cold in the Earth' learns to cherish existence 'without the aid of joy', and 'The Stoic' to love only liberty. Although there are many poems of suffering, there are few of personal weakness or uncertainty; 'If grief for grief can touch thee', and the sad lines on her brother Branwell in 'The Wanderer from the Fold', are among the few which do not find some resolution in courage or mystical experience.

Emily's work in both poetry and prose is much taken up with opposites and their resolution. The 'three rivers' in 'The Philosopher' seem to represent a strife of opposing forces which can be resolved only by the 'spirit, seer'. The central, passion-torn triangle of the Gondal characters (Julius, Augusta, Aspin) is echoed in the two generations of *Wuthering Heights*, whose conflicts are only resolved in the love of Catherine and Hareton. There are many reverberations between the novel and the poems, and speculation can easily run wild; but Lockwood's dream seems to be anticipated in 'A sudden chasm'; Heathcliff's longing to lie in the earth with Cathy in 'A thousand sounds of happiness'; Cathy's identity with Heathcliff in 'No coward soul'; and Cathy's conflict between Edgar and Heathcliff in the poem 'Stars'.

Style

The simple purity of Emily's style is remarkable at a time which was beginning to admire the luscious Romantic manner of John Keats (1795-1821), Shelley and the young Tennyson (1809-92), and their followers. As in her prose, she always prefers the concrete image to the abstract, and she uses this imagery skilfully, to convey and concentrate a high intensity of feeling. Her manner varies little over the ten years or so in which she wrote most of her verse. Certain of the more troubling themes become more dominant, but the style and expression alter little. The fine poem, 'The night is darkening', was written when she was only nineteen, and her characteristic voice and skill are already there. There are no youthful, intimate outpourings; from the beginning the poet in Emily transformed her personal suffering (or that of her characters) into a statement of universal meaning.

She is rarely a narrative poet, and her chief strength lies in the brief lyrical, elegiac, or ballad form. There is evidence not only in the poems themselves, but in her notes and fragments, that she was a very deliberate craftsman, who planned carefully. Few of the poems are inventive in metre, but in almost all of them the variations in rhythm, stress, and vowel-sounds delicately reflect what the verses hope to convey. Assonance and alliteration are used deftly, with a strict attention to relevance. One verse from 'The Death of A.G.A.' is enough to show these skills:

At last the sunshine left the ground;
The laden bee flew home;
The deep down sea, with sadder sound,
Impelled its waves to foam.

Although the language of the poems is so confident, it is (surprisingly) very much less metaphorical than the prose of *Wuthering Heights*. In its deceptive simplicity it makes little use of the condensation of metaphor and simile. Much of the imagery is taken from nature. Storms and snow are much drawn upon, and 'Last Lines' and 'Tell me' are among many of the poems in which the sea is used as an image of the infinite and eternal. As in *Wuthering Heights*, much imagery is taken from rock and stone, and in several poems, such as 'The Prisoner' ('Ah, sooner might the sun thaw down these granite stones') the stone is that of a prison wall. Other images, more minutely observed, include 'The dark moss dripping from the wall', 'The dim moon struggling in the sky', 'The blue ice curdling on the stream'. In 'The Outcast Mother' the lines 'Forests of heather, dark and long/Wave their brown branching arms above' convey with perfect economy the upward view of the baby on the ground.

The sympathetic influence of Wordsworth and Shelley on Emily's themes has already been mentioned. The most obvious influence on her style is also that of Wordsworth, whose diction and verse-forms are frequently echoed in her work. The language she chooses for her writing aspires to exactly the kind of poetic language advocated by Wordsworth in his Preface to the *Lyrical Ballads*. Several of the other poets who influenced her thought, such as Scott, also had their effect on her style. Many of the poems are reminiscent of William Blake (1757-1827), but it is thought she cannot have known his work. The voracious reading of the Brontës was wholly adapted to their own purposes, but it had its effect on much of their work.

Charlotte's view

When Charlotte first came accidentally upon Emily's poems, she was astonished. They stirred her 'like the sound of a trumpet', and in 1850 she wrote, 'I thought them condensed and terse, vigorous and genuine. To my ear they had also a peculiar music – wild, melancholy, and elevating'. She may have had a sister's partiality, but her view still stands.

PLATE 5: Anne, by Charlotte, in watercolour.

Part 4

Anne Brontë

Her life (1820–1849)

The Brontës moved into the parsonage at Haworth in 1820, three months after Anne was born. She was the youngest of the family of six, and she was always frail and asthmatic. Her mother died of cancer the next year, and she and Branwell became the favourites of Aunt Branwell, who came to live with them. Because she was too young, she escaped the horror of the Clergy Daughters' School at Cowan Bridge, which all her sisters attended. Maria and Elizabeth, the two eldest, died of tuberculosis soon after their return from this school in 1825, and Anne's relationship with Emily became, and remained, very close. It is probable that the first serious efforts at writing and drawing by Charlotte and Branwell were done to amuse Anne.

All her life Anne seems to have been gentle and pious, and much beloved by family and friends. She read and learned as eagerly as her sisters, played the piano, and (like all the Brontës) sketched and drew skilfully. When she was seven, she was given her due share in the 'plays' which developed into the Glass Town saga (see 'Unpublished writings', pp.23–6). Later, in 1831 or soon after, she and Emily abandoned the epic of Glass Town, which was being ever expanded by Charlotte and Branwell, and began to construct their own long romance of Gondal – a task which occupied them, intermittently, until nearly the end of their lives. How much of the Gondal story (now lost, except for its poems) was written by Anne and how much by Emily can never be known, but even if Emily's was the larger share, Anne was still deeply involved.

In 1835, when Emily left Roe Head after a term, Anne took her place as a free pupil. Charlotte was then a teacher there, but she was cut off from Anne by her position, and by her own depression at the time. Although thought to be so delicate, Anne was successful in her school work, and much liked by her fellows, but in 1836 she too became depressed and ill. She underwent a deep religious crisis, believing herself to be one of the damned, cut off from the love of God. (See 'Religion and the Church', pp.15–17). A minister was brought to see her, and he gradually restored her confidence in mercy and forgiveness. Her health, however, continued to deteriorate, and in 1837 her father brought her home for good. For much of 1838 she was at home with her sisters, and probably deeply engaged in stories of Gondal.

She was the first of the family to venture to become a governess. Like her sisters, she wished to relieve her father of expense, and to attain a degree of independence. In 1839 she took up a post with the Ingham family in Yorkshire, but she could not control the unruly children, received no support from their parents, and was dismissed after eight months. This searing experience later found fictional expression in *Agnes Grey*.

1840 was marked by her sisters' companionship at home, and by the presence of her father's new curate, William Weightman, a charming and flirtatious man, much liked by the whole family. It seems that in the course of the year Anne fell in love with him, but he did not respond, and in 1841 she took another position as governess with the Robinson family at Thorp Green Hall. Here again she suffered all the humiliations which she and Charlotte were later to chronicle so thoroughly. She was considered socially inferior, ignored by the family, and given no encouragement in her attempts to teach and discipline the children who were her charges. She was lonely and discouraged, but she persevered, and when she found time, expanded the Gondal story and continued with her own studies, especially in Latin, German, and music. In 1841 she joined her sisters in devising a plan for a school to be run at the parsonage, but she continued at Thorp Green when they went to Brussels.

Two hard blows fell in 1842; Branwell was dismissed from his job on the railway, where he seemed to be doing well at last; and the curate, William Weightman, died. In a poem on his death, she described him as 'The lightest heart that I have known/The kindest I shall ever know'.

She persuaded her employers (though it must have been with some misgivings) to employ Branwell as a tutor for their son, and he joined her at Thorp Green early in 1843. The Robinsons presented Anne with a spaniel, Flossy, who was much loved and sketched by her and Emily. The prospectus for the school was published in 1844, and Anne was probably the most dispirited of the sisters when there were no replies. She had never been happy at Thorp Green, and the prospect of the school offered excitement and release. Besides this, Branwell's drinking and his flirtation with Mrs Robinson (whom he believed to be deeply enamoured of him) were increasingly embarrassing. She resigned her post in 1845, and Branwell was dismissed from his in the same year.

Anne was still involved in the Gondal saga, and when she and Emily made a jaunt to York together in 1845 they were still developing and enacting their Gondal characters. To Emily they were still very real, but to Anne their charm was fading. She had begun her first serious adult writing with *Passages in the Life of an Individual* (later transformed into *Agnes Grey*), and henceforth her interest was to be in writing based on her own experience.

A selection of her poems was included with Charlotte's and Emily's in the book assembled by Charlotte, and published in 1846 as *Poems by Currer, Ellis and Acton Bell* (Charlotte, Emily, and Anne). The book sold only two copies, and the only favourable public comment was on Emily's work. In the same year the sisters sent to a round of publishers three manuscript novels: *The Professor*, by Charlotte, *Wuthering Heights*, by Emily, and *Agnes Grey*, by Anne. Emily's and Anne's books were eventually accepted in the summer of 1847, but publication did not proceed. It was not until the success of Charlotte's *Jane Eyre* in the autumn of 1847 that Emily's and Anne's books appeared. In the agitation which accompanied the publication of *Jane Eyre* and *Wuthering Heights*, Anne's work was little noticed, but one reviewer accused it of exaggeration and 'over-colouring'.

Meanwhile Anne was suffering from recurring asthma, and she had become deeply depressed by Branwell's decline into drink and drugs, and by his wild imaginings about himself and Mrs Robinson. She felt it her duty to write a novel with a strong moralistic bent, on the horror of a drunken and profligate life, and in 1846 she began *The Tenant of Wildfell Hall*. It was published in 1848 and received considerable attention, but little praise. Reviewers considered that it was coarse and revelled in debauchery.

In the autumn of that year Branwell died, and in December Emily followed. Anne knew her own health was threatened, but she had faith in her determination to live. She went to London with Charlotte, to straighten out a confusion between their publishers, and later they went together to York and Scarborough. She hoped the sea air would cure her, for she longed 'to do some good in the world'. But she was dying of tuberculosis, which had already taken three of her sisters, and she died in Scarborough in May. To save their father's distress, Charlotte had her buried there, in a graveyard overlooking the shore.

Writings

Anne has always been overshadowed by her sisters, but there are signs that her qualities are now being more generally recognised. Like her sisters, she served a long apprenticeship in writing before she published. For years she had been contributing to the elaborate structure of romance, intrigue and adventure that made up the Gondal stories.

The wild and stormy island of Gondal seems to have sprung from the climate of Yorkshire, while its companion, Gaaldine, was lush and warm. Some of Anne's Gondal poems, describing 'sweet blue-bells' or 'the frost-winds', seem to describe her own local haunts. In 1832-3 she wrote out two lists of Gondal characters and place-names, and these have given vital clues to the lost prose story. As her interest in Gondal waned, she began to write of her own experience and the real life of everyday. By the time *Passages in the Life of an Individual* was recast as *Agnes Grey*, Gondal had served its purpose for her.

She published only two novels, the one-volume *Agnes Grey* and the two-volume *The Tenant of Wildfell Hall.* When she finished the latter she was still only twenty-eight, two years younger than Charlotte when she wrote *The Professor*, and already in judgement, control of material, and general good sense she was Charlotte's peer. Her writing lacks the fire and intensity of her sisters' work, but she has clarity, precision, uncompromising honesty, and the family skill in the use of exact, concrete imagery. Like them, she wrote of what she saw and felt, and did not sacrifice this integrity for easy success.

Although she read avidly in both poetry and prose, and knew the Gothic and romantic literature of her time, she seems to have had no problem in avoiding romantic excess. Her gaze is steady and penetrating, and there is no lack of sharp comment or ironic humour – at its best, reminiscent of Jane Austen. She was probably the best educated of the three highly educated sisters. She attended Roe Head School for over two years, complementing her long home education, and she was probably the most accomplished drawer and painter of the three very accomplished girls. In spite of her asthma, and her poor general health, she was full of resolution; she was the first of the three to become a governess, and the first to extricate herself from fantasy in order to write serious, realistic work. The novelist and critic George Moore (1852-1933) considered her 'the greatest of the Brontës'. Although this judgement seems merely perverse, her writing and her attitudes are so reminiscent of her sisters, it is not surprising some contemporaries supposed Currer, Ellis, and Acton Bell to be one and the same person.

Agnes Grey

Summary

Agnes's father, a parson, had married a well-to-do young woman, whose parents disapproved of the match. Trying to improve his family's finances, he loses all his money. Agnes, by then eighteen, determines to become a governess, an occupation she feels she will greatly enjoy.

She arrives at Wellwood, the mansion of her employers, the Bloomfields. Mrs Bloomfield is cold, the children quarrelsome. Tom, a boy of seven, boasts of torturing small animals, and his younger sister is jealous and demanding. The coarse, bullying Mr Bloomfield terrifies his children into good behaviour, but away from him they are turbulent and vicious. Agnes is in despair, yet determined to prove herself. The adults of the family, and their friends, humiliate and ignore her, and encourage Tom in his drinking, swearing, and cruelty. Just as she feels she is making a little progress, she is dismissed.

Happy as she is at home, she is nevertheless determined to find another post, and takes employment with Mr and Mrs Murray of Horton Lodge, a fine country mansion. The children are older than the Bloomfields, but in their way just as troublesome. Rosalie is beautiful and frivolous, Matilda a horse-mad tomboy. There are also two boys, both difficult, but fortunately they are soon sent away to school. Again Agnes is made to feel the lowliness of her position, but she is determined to remain, and Rosalie, though insolent and patronising, becomes fond of her.

Agnes's sister, Mary, is to be married to a parson (a fate which appals Rosalie) and Agnes leaves Horton to attend the wedding. When she returns Rosalie has had her coming-out ball, and met the rich, profligate baronet, Sir Thomas Ashby, whom she supposes she will marry. In passing, she mentions the arrival of an ugly new curate, Mr Weston. At church Agnes is much impressed with Weston, especially in contrast with the vain and worldly parson, Mr Hatfield. She takes to visiting the local cottagers, and hears from an old widow, Nancy Brown, about the kindness shown her by Mr Weston. Agnes is intensely lonely, sometimes in despair, but Mr Weston's presence in the village gives her hope. She meets him accidentally in Nancy's cottage, then later he catches up with her after church; they pick some primroses, and she talks of her home. He says it is possible to be useful and happy on one's own, as he is.

Rosalie has been amusing herself by enslaving Mr Hatfield, but scornfully rejects his proposal of marriage. Obliquely, Agnes confesses to the reader her love for Mr Weston, but at that point Rosalie decides he will be her new conquest. Agnes suffers deeply as she watches Rosalie's attempts to ensnare him. Although she regards herself as having no beauty or charm, she begins to take pains with her dress, and reflects sadly on the fact that (whatever moralists say) in matters of love, beauty is indeed important.

Rosalie becomes engaged to Sir Thomas Ashby, but wishes to postpone her wedding to permit more time for coquetry. She continues her attempts to enslave Mr Weston, and in the middle of her anguish at watching these events, Agnes hears her father is very ill. At last, to her great agitation, she encounters Mr Weston, who asks after Rosalie, but gives Agnes a large bunch of bluebells, making her wonderfully happy. When she arrives home she finds her father has died.

Agnes, together with her mother and sister, decides that she will open a small school. Her grandfather says he will help if their mother repents of her marriage, but they all agree she must not do this. Agnes returns to Horton, to hand in her notice. For two weeks she does not see Mr Weston except in church. When they meet by chance he asks about her home, and if she would mind if they never met again. She is greatly moved, and cannot prevent her tears.

Agnes and her mother work busily at their school, but she longs for a letter from Weston. After some months she becomes listless and ill. A letter from Rosalie, now Lady Ashby, invites her for a visit. Ashby Park is magnificent, but Rosalie keeps Agnes away from the family. She is very discontented, and is enjoying flirtations in London. Agnes is appalled, and distressed to hear that Mr Weston has left Horton.

Her school is in a small seaside town, and early one summer morning she goes walking on the sands. Suddenly Mr Weston is before her. He has a parish nearby, and has been looking for her. Her confusion is so great she cannot respond sensibly, but says he may call at the house. He becomes a regular visitor, and one fine summer evening asks her to marry him. A few weeks later they are married, and embark on a full and happy life.

General commentary

It seems that Anne was writing her *Passages in the Life of an Individual*, based on her experiences as a governess, before either Charlotte or Emily had emerged from their fantasies of Angria and Gondal. By July 1846 she had recast it as *Agnes Grey*, but along with Charlotte's *The Professor* and Emily's *Wuthering Heights*, it was rejected many times before it was finally published in December 1847. Anne and Emily both had to contribute fifty pounds (a large sum in those days) before T.C. Newby would publish.

Anne's attitude towards her writing was more moral and instructional than that of her sisters. The first sentence of *Agnes Grey* reads, 'All true histories contain instruction', and in her Preface to the second edition of *The Tenant of Wildfell Hall* she makes plain her intention to instruct and reform. This does not mean that she explicitly points the moral, or turns her stories into didactic tracts. Her method is to tell her tale without comment or disguise, and leave her readers to draw their own conclusions.

Agnes Grey has the odd distinction of being the only one of the Brontë novels in which the heroine has a mother who is part of her life throughout her story (Caroline Helstone, in Charlotte's *Shirley*, does not discover her mother until she is a young woman).

The benign influence of the poet William Cowper (1731-1800), and especially of his poem 'The Task', is apparent in Anne's feeling for wild and domestic animals, in her dislike of fox-hunting, and in Edward

Weston, her model of all a parson should be. George Moore proclaimed *Agnes Grey* to be 'the most perfect prose narrative in English Literature'. Again his judgement seems over-enthusiastic, but it does indicate that the economy, unity, and charm of this small work should be taken seriously.

Plot and structure

The plot is straightforward and the structure simple. The early scenes, establishing Agnes's background, are told swiftly and economically. In the first quarter of the book Agnes is engaged largely with small children, the Bloomfields, and in the rest of the story with older and adolescent children, the Murrays. With the second family her relationships develop, both in the house and in the neighbourhood, until she has to leave when her father dies. She and her mother then open a little seaside school, when Mr Weston rediscovers her. Unlike all other Brontë novels, a happy home and family circle are always in the background.

The narration is in the first person, direct and seemingly artless, with little of the subtlety of Charlotte or Emily, or their skill in introducing other views in a first-person narrative. The attitudes of the Bloomfields, the Murrays, and Mr Weston are conveyed solely through Agnes's description of conversations and incidents, and occasionally through letters. There are, however, various touches of contrivance; Mr Weston's devotion, for instance, is carefully concealed from the reader, as it is from Agnes.

Although so much of the book is based on Anne's experience, the real and the fictitious are neatly carpentered, and readers who knew nothing of Anne's life could not tell which part was which. The happy ending to the love-story, the presence of Agnes's mother, the father's death, and the story of Rosalie are among the fictional parts. In her Preface to the second edition of *The Tenant of Wildfell Hall*, Anne describes how reviewers had refused to credit those very parts of *Agnes Grey* which had been 'carefully copied from the life'.

Themes

The theme of instruction and reform has already been touched upon. If, in Anne's words, 'All true histories contain instruction', what was it she wished to impart? The problem of a woman's place in society, which so preoccupied Charlotte, is reflected in Agnes's history of employment as a governess. In describing Agnes's experiences with the Bloomfields and the Murrays, Anne has a double theme; she intends to expose the degrading treatment meted out to governesses, and at the same time to show how the girls in their charge are brought up to think only of 'accomplishments' and a wealthy marriage. As a governess, Agnes is snubbed, ignored, and given no support in her efforts to encourage study and discipline; her charges are taught to despise her, and to think only of a future of affluence and pleasure. In an exchange worthy of Jane Austen, Rosalie questions Agnes about her sister's marriage:

> 'Is he rich?'
> 'No – only comfortable.'
> 'Is he handsome?'
> 'No – only decent.'
> 'Young?'
> 'No – only middling.'
> 'Oh mercy! what a wretch!'

In those few words her marriage theme is neatly exposed.

The comfort of the Murrays' life at Horton Lodge is strongly contrasted with the life of the poor in the nearby village, and Anne's theme of compassion for the unfortunate is firmly emphasised by the kindness of Agnes and Mr Weston, and the indifference and condescension of Mr Hatfield and the Murrays. The rheumatic old Nancy Brown is despised by the Murray girls, whose consciences are easily allayed by occasional visits, and she is contemptuously dismissed by Mr Hatfield as 'a canting old fool'.

The contrast between Edward Weston and his superior, Mr Hatfield, points to a lesson in church reform. Like her father, Anne had no time for fashionable, ambitious clergy, interested only in the wealthy people of the neighbourhood, and Mr Weston is carefully modelled on the kind of curate the Brontës believed the church should encourage.

Another evident contrast is between the warm security of home and the harsh realities of the world outside. This distinction was felt strongly by the home-loving Brontës in their everyday lives, but it is expressed most vividly in fiction in this story by Anne.

Style

Anne's writing is simple and direct. It does not share the driving vigour of her sisters' prose, and it is considerably less charged with metaphor and image, but nevertheless it is neatly adapted to its purpose. There are sentences of enormous length, such as the description of Rosalie in Chapter 7, but they are broken up with semi-colons, and interspersed with brief, even abrupt, lines. The whole reads easily and naturally, like good conversation. There is indeed a great deal of conversation in Anne's work, always lively and natural, without the affectation sometimes found in Charlotte's attempts. Rosalie rattles on, Agnes replies, and the reader seems almost to be overhearing them. Anne's ear for the flow of everyday speech is probably the best of all the Brontës.

There are no long descriptions of landscape or weather, and Anne is very conscious that she aims to write with economy. 'I cannot, like Dogberry, find it in my heart to bestow *all* my tediousness upon the reader', she says, and her few brief descriptions are all done with vivid economy, and skilfully placed in Agnes's narrative; when she is deeply depressed at Ashby Park, with her life 'drab-colour', she watches the rooks at twilight and her sadness is deepened by seeing the night close in on them, in the same way that darkness of spirit is closing in on her. Her description of the sea, the pools, the seaweed, and the sand, on the walk during which Weston finds her, is not only sharp and fresh, it is possibly the first description in English literature of a morning walk on the beach.

Most of Agnes's life is far from amusing, but there are moments of humour – ironic, acerbic, or simply amused – and these, too, are tightly and economically accomplished. Matilda Murray's tomboy antics are robustly comical; there is much ironic humour in Rosalie's letter inviting Agnes to Ashby Park; and poor Agnes is all too well aware of the exhibition she makes of herself in trying to eat the tough, cold meat served by Mrs Bloomfield.

Characters

Agnes: She is all excited innocence when she decides to go out into the world and teach – 'delightful task!' she exclaims. But there is little to delight her in the wild, vicious Bloomfield children; she is sickened by the red-faced coarseness of Mr Bloomfield, and depressed by the family's contemptuous treatment of her. She begins to believe that she herself was brought up with too much kindness to have acquired sufficient independence. However, she shows great courage, and is determined to prove herself; her dismissal does not break her, but spurs her on to try again. Throughout her trials she behaves with an attractive, quiet dignity, crushed neither by the turbulence of the children nor by the criticism of their parents. In spite of their great differences, Rosalie becomes genuinely fond of her, rather as Ginevra becomes fond of Lucy in Charlotte's *Villette*.

She comes nearest to despair when she realises she loves Mr Weston, and he seems to notice only the flirtatious Rosalie. She is tormented with jealousy, and this only increases the guilt she already feels for loving him 'with the service of a heart more bent upon the creature than upon the Creator' (a guilt also shared by Charlotte's heroines, Jane Eyre and Lucy Snowe).

Agnes is a reserved young woman, keeping her troubles to herself and confiding in no-one. She does not even confide over-much in the reader, preferring to allow the facts and her own mood to speak for themselves. At Horton she suffers acute loneliness, but her isolation, and her anguish at the apparent loss of Weston, is expressed more in her depression and dogged perseverance than in a flow of tears or words.

Her tenderness towards her family, and even towards the children who torment her, is very much part of her character. She loves animals, and is greatly touched by Weston's rescue of Nancy's cat, for she believes (as do Charlotte's Shirley and Caroline) that gentleness to animals reveals a kind heart. She makes her disapproval plain when Matilda enjoys the spectacle of her terrier killing a young hare.

The reader knows little of Agnes's appearance, and her brief comments are all deprecating – as when she sees, on arriving at the Bloomfields, that the wind had 'dyed her face of a pale purple'. The impression emerges that she looks pleasant and neat, but her extreme modesty about her own attractions makes it impossible for her to believe that Mr Weston is indeed singling her out. She is by no means the most exciting, but she is one of the most pleasing of all the Brontë heroines.

Edward Weston: He is almost certainly largely modelled on William Weightman, one of Mr Brontë's curates with whom, it seems, Anne fell in love (see 'Life', pp.123–5). In every respect the perfect curate and parson, he is devout, serious, hard-working, sensitive to the needs of others, and reflective. When he obtains his own parish, he sets about reforming and reorganising it. He is not immune to the flattery of the beautiful Rosalie, but he is not deceived by it, and he loves Agnes long before he declares himself. The scene in which he gathers the three primroses for her is a touching episode of tremulous, undeclared love. Agnes notices with pleasure and approval how he strokes Nancy's cat as it sits on his knee, instead of kicking it away as Mr Hatfield does. For Agnes, he represents all that can make marriage secure and happy.

Mr Hatfield: There is very little to be said in his favour. He is a dandy, who wears a diamond ring, curls his hair, and attends only to the wealthy and powerful, among whom he intends to make a rich marriage. He despises the poor, and threatens Nancy Brown with damnation if she does not come to church. His sermons are arid discourses, and the God he serves is not a loving Father but 'a terrible taskmaster'. To amuse herself, Rosalie contrives to make him fall in love with her, then rejects him with malicious scorn.

The Bloomfields: Mrs Bloomfield is cold and critical to Agnes, indulgent to her dreadful children, and at odds with her husband. He is coarse in his habits, bullying in his manner, and undermines all Agnes's attempts to reform the selfish, violent young Tom, on the grounds that swearing, drinking, and torturing animals will 'make a man of him'. There are many resemblances to the Inghams of Blake Hall, where Anne first worked as a governess (see 'Life', pp.123–5).

The Murrays: Again, there are strong similarities between some of the Murrays (notably Mrs Murray and her daughter Rosalie) and the Robinsons of Thorp Green Hall, Anne's second employers. Mrs Murray wishes only for pretty looks and showy accomplishments in her daughters, leading to wealthy marriages. Rosalie willingly follows her mother's prescription, and becomes 'swallowed up in the all-absorbing ambition to attract and dazzle'. Her sister Matilda, however, rebels against her upbringing, and becomes a rumbustious tomboy, disgusted with ladylike indoor pursuits, and no more inclined to learn her lessons than Rosalie. Their father's red face, noisy laughter, and general ferocity and greed do not endear him to Agnes.

The Tenant of Wildfell Hall

Summary

The novel is cast in the form of a letter and a journal. In the first part of the book Gilbert Markham, a well-to-do young farmer, writes in 1827 to his brother-in-law, Halford, of events which had taken place twenty years before.

At tea, he and his mother and siblings talk about the new tenant of Wildfell Hall, a fine local house owned by Mr Frederick Lawrence. The new tenant is a Mrs Graham, a beautiful and mysterious young widow with a young son, Arthur. Gilbert rescues the boy from a fall, and is intrigued by his mother, Mrs Graham, but finds her reserved. He is anyway engaged in a flirtation with Eliza, the vicar's daughter. On a visit to the Markhams Mrs Graham will not allow the boy to sip wine, and explains that she is teaching him to dislike it.

On a visit to her, Gilbert discovers she is a professional painter, and he comes upon a portrait of a handsome, dissolute-looking young man. He devises plans to waylay Mrs Graham out walking, but Mr Lawrence obliquely warns him to beware. In the village Eliza, now aware of Gilbert's new attraction, hints that Mrs Graham is the mistress of Mr Lawrence, and Arthur is their son.

Gilbert declares his love, and malicious gossip prompts the vicar to reprimand Mrs Graham. Gilbert finds her distraught and begs her to marry him, but she refuses and says she will explain the next day. As he lingers nearby, he hears her and Mr Lawrence talking affectionately, and begins to believe the gossip. Desperately unhappy, he ignores her, and when Mr Lawrence tries to speak reasonably to him he attacks him with his whip. Helen Graham is angry with him, but gives him her journal to read in explanation.

The second section of the novel consists of Helen's journal, which was begun six years before. Helen is back in the country with her uncle and aunt, having just completed a season of parties in London, where she had met the wild, captivating Arthur Huntingdon. A few months later her uncle entertains a shooting-party, which includes Huntingdon, his friend Lord Lowborough, and the flirtatious Annabella Wilmot. Huntingdon pains Helen by his attentions to Annabella, but soon proposes marriage to Helen. Helen's aunt implores her to remember Huntingdon's unsavoury reputation, but Helen is wholly confident she can reform him. Huntingdon boasts of how he has depraved Lowborough with gambling and drink, and Helen is shaken to hear that Annabella is marrying Lowborough only for his title.

Writing two months after her marriage, Helen confesses her disappointment. She is now mistress of Grassdale Manor, but feels she is only a pretty toy to her husband, who continues with his selfish dissipations. She expects a child, but when her husband returns from London after three months away he is irritable and ill from his riotous life. He entertains a shooting-party, which includes the Lowboroughs, and Helen is distressed by his attentions to Annabella. Mrs Hargrave, who has a son, Walter, and two daughters, Millicent and Esther, has contrived to marry Millicent to the wealthy reprobate, Hattersley, and now plans that Esther shall also marry for money.

Helen's son, Arthur, is born, and soon becomes everything to her, for her marriage is dead and Huntingdon is almost always in London. The young Esther Hargrave greatly charms Helen, but she is disturbed by the attentions of Walter. Huntingdon returns, constantly abusive and drunk, and when Helen's father dies he will not allow her to go to the funeral. His friends come to visit, and scenes of violent drunkenness take place. Walter and Lowborough, however, remain aloof. Helen overhears two guests complaining that Huntingdon is being reformed by a woman, and she joyfully embraces him, supposing the woman to be herself, but Walter tells her that her husband is conducting a love-affair with Lady Lowborough. Helen sees them together and accuses him, but he refuses to set her free or return her property. She tells Lady Lowborough to go, and is horrified to find that all Huntingdon's friends assume Walter is her lover.

Husband and wife now live as strangers, while Huntingdon indulges and spoils his son. Walter protests his love, but Helen angrily refuses to become his mistress. After five years of marriage she is determined to leave, taking Arthur with her. In order to obtain some money of her own, she works at her painting, but Huntingdon discovers her plan to escape, and proceeds to destroy her paintings and lock up her jewels. When he again leaves for London, Helen tries to remedy the harm he has done to their son with his encouragement of drinking and swearing. She asks her brother, Frederick, if he will allow her and Arthur to live in Wildfell Hall, their old childhood home. When Huntingdon returns to Grassdale, he brings a new governess, who is also his mistress. Helen packs her few things, and, with Arthur and her faithful servant, Rachel, leaves secretly.

Using the name of Mrs Graham, she settles at Wildfell Hall, pretending that Frederick is only her landlord. She tries to allay the curiosity of the village by paying calls, and meets Gilbert. At this point the journal ends. Markham's letter, which began the book, now continues. He reads Helen's journal and begs her forgiveness. They embrace, and he says he will wait for her husband's death. Meanwhile Helen feels she must leave again, in order to escape Huntingdon's enquiries.

After many months, Gilbert hears to his astonishment that Helen has returned to nurse Huntingdon, who has had a bad fall from his horse. She nurses him patiently, trying to overcome his terror of death, and he becomes alternately abusive and clinging. She is determined that he will never again have charge of Arthur. Huntingdon insists on drinking again, his wound becomes gangrenous, and he dies in great fear and pain.

Helen is now very wealthy, and sadly Gilbert realises how unequal they are in rank and fortune. Eventually he is told that Helen is to marry Walter Hargrave, and that Frederick will be at the wedding. Appalled, he makes a long winter journey through the snow to Grassdale, and arrives in time to see that the bride is not Helen, but Esther Hargrave, and the groom is Frederick. When he arrives at Grassdale Manor he finds Helen has gone, and pursues her to her aunt's at Stanningley. On his journey he finds out that her uncle has left her most of his fortune, and she is wealthier than ever. Feeling his case is hopeless, he is about to go when he encounters Helen by the gate and is invited into the house. Eventually he convinces her that it was only her wealth that kept him away, and soon after they are married. When young Arthur is grown up, he marries and settles at Grassdale Manor.

The writing of *The Tenant of Wildfell Hall*

Anne's intention of writing a moral tale was clearly expressed in her Preface to the second edition, written in July 1848. The novel had been castigated for its 'coarseness' and scenes of drunken brutality, and Anne felt it necessary to defend herself. 'I wished to tell the truth,' she wrote, 'for truth always conveys its own moral...'. She shared the Brontë devotion to honesty, and stated that 'when we have to do with vice and vicious characters...it is better to depict them as they really are'. She continued, 'when I feel it my duty to speak an unpalatable truth...I *will* speak it, though it be to the prejudice of my name'.

She chose this story, and followed it through to its scenes of terror and death, because she wished to give her own warning to the world about the horrors of over-indulgence in drink. She had before her the painful example of her brother Branwell, whose drinking, she believed, was the chief cause of his tragic decline. In Charlotte's 'Biographical Notice' to the 1850 edition of the novels, she describes Anne's horror and depression at Branwell's fate. 'She brooded over it,' Charlotte wrote, 'till she believed it to be a duty to reproduce every detail...as a warning to others.' Anne did not intend to write a didactic tract (for 'truth always conveys its own moral'), and she did not wish to ban alcohol; but she did feel it her earnest duty to show, through a story, what over-indulgence might do.

Helen's marriage to Huntingdon has a probable source in a visit to the Brontë parsonage of an unknown woman, who came to ask Mr Brontë's advice. Her husband was a drunken bully, and Mr Brontë (much against the convention of the time) advised her to leave him. Charlotte touched upon the topic in *The Professor*, when Mrs Edward Crimsworth leaves her husband, but Anne put this agonised decision at the heart of her novel. Her experiences with the Robinsons at Thorp Green Hall may also have provided ideas for her story; at the Hall, she wrote, she had encountered 'some very unpleasant...experience of human nature'. It is also likely that Thomas Moore's biography of Lord Byron, which is thought to have influenced Emily, had its effect on Anne as well in providing a model of a turbulent, profligate life.

The novel is vastly more ambitious than *Agnes Grey*, in scope, intent, and organisation. Technically it must be seen as a great advance, and in creative drive and invention it far outstrips its charming predecessor. The last chapters, in particular, have an imaginative force worthy of Charlotte or Emily.

Plot and structure

The plot itself is simple; Helen marries Huntingdon, leads a disastrously unhappy life with him, has a son, leaves her husband, meets Markham, returns to nurse Huntingdon on his death-bed, and after his death marries Markham. Excitement and mystery are maintained to the end, when the reader is led to share Markham's belief that he has lost Helen to Hargrave.

The structure, however, is far from simple. It is organised in such a way that suspense is maintained, and that the many characters and families who populate the book are kept distinct and individual. The two main stories, of Helen's involvement first with Huntingdon and then with Markham, are kept deliberately apart by the structure within which they occur.

Anne chose two traditional conventions of the novel, both much employed in the eighteen century – the letter and the diary. Her entire story is in fact told in retrospect by Helen's second husband, Markham, who relates the events known to him in a series of letters to his brother-in-law, Halford. The events of Helen's earlier life, leading up to her meeting with Markham, are described by her in a journal, or diary, which she lends Markham, and which he copies out for the benefit of Halford. Thus the novel divides into three parts: Chapters 1-26 consist of Markham's letters to Halford, and describe his growing friendship and love for the mysterious tenant of the Hall; Chapters 26-44 contain Helen's journal of her previous life; Chapters 45-53 revert again to Markham's letters, describing events from the time Helen lent him her journal. The first section admirably poses the mystery of 'Mrs Graham', as observed by the puzzled Markham; the second explains much of the mystery, but not all; the third sustains suspense through Helen's absence, first with Huntingdon, then with her aunt, and through Markham's misinformation about Helen's remarriage.

The device of letters and journal, and of the unknown recipient, Halford, is, of course, wholly incredible. Nevertheless, if this convention can be forgotten or accepted, it is a small price to pay for an ingenious and successful narrative construction.

Themes

The theme of drinking and its horrors has already been touched upon. Huntingdon and his friends drink to excess, and their most violent actions are performed under its influence. Huntingdon's depravity, however, is not entirely caused by alcohol. His character is selfish and profligate long before his drinking begins to take its terrible effect. Drink accentuates the moral weakness that is already there, and precipitates him into a headlong decline. Characters of some moral strength, such as Lawrence and Markham, can take drink as it should be taken, moderately. But those who are in any way weak and self-indulgent, such as Huntingdon and Hattersley, are in danger of succumbing, with tragic results. Helen's experience of drink has been so terrible that when she comes to live at Wildfell Hall her violent aversion to drink causes comment in the village.

Like Charlotte, Anne was much concerned with the position of women in marriage and in society. When the Brontës were writing, and until the Married Women's Property Act of 1882, a woman and all she owned became her husband's property on marriage. It was therefore very difficult for a woman to leave an unsatisfactory husband. And not only was it difficult, it was considered an immoral act. Helen is able to leave Huntingdon only because of her talent for painting, and because she has her brother's help in finding somewhere to live. Millicent Hattersley, in a similar predicament, miserably submits to her fate. The author's sympathy with Helen's action in leaving is made plain, just as Charlotte's sympathy is given to the absconding Mrs Crimsworth (P).

The difficulties of married love are exposed not only in the Huntingdons, but in the Lowboroughs. Lord Lowborough marries the fascinating Annabella, only to find that she is indulging in a love-affair with Huntingdon; later he remarries, this time a middle-aged woman of good sense, warmth and cheerfulness, more suited to marriage in every way. Like Charlotte, Anne seems to have felt that the state of being 'in love' was not necessarily the best basis for marriage. The double standard by which a husband may enjoy love affairs while his wife may not, is even further extended when Huntingdon offers his wife to anyone who wants her, and then rounds on her for her supposed infidelity.

The familiar Brontë interest in social status finds expression in Markham's despairing belief that Helen is too far above him in wealth and rank. But he finds that Helen – like Charlotte's Shirley – holds these barriers to be of no importance if love is strong.

Anne's tendency to a belief in the Calvinist doctrines of hell and damnation (see 'Religion and the Church', pp.15–17) showed itself in her acute depression at Roe Head in 1836 (see 'Life', pp.123–5), and it is again apparent in *The Tenant of Wildfell Hall*. Helen marries Arthur not only because she falls in love, but because she fervently believes she can reform and save him. When she finds she cannot, she begins to fear that he is damned and destined for hell. Although she nurses him at his death, and does what she can to comfort his fears and persuade him to repent, his refusal means she cannot be certain he will be immediately received in heaven, even though she believes he will ultimately be forgiven.

In both her novels, Anne shows great interest in the bringing up of children. In *Agnes Grey* the brutalising of little Tom, who is encouraged to drink and swear, and the indulgence given to the violent conduct of the Murray boys, is repeated in Huntingdon's attempts to corrupt his young son. Anne is clear that too much praise and latitude must be avoided. The Brontë girls apparently felt that their father had over-praised and over-indulged Branwell, and it is noticeable that neither Agnes nor Helen believes in spoiling or giving way to their charges. Helen is insistent that when Arthur is old enough he must work at a regular occupation.

Style

As in *Agnes Grey*, the writing is clear and fluent, with variation in length and pace, but little reliance on metaphor and image. It is always relevant and controlled, and again there is a considerable amount of conversation, most of which conveys attitude, feeling, and information with economy and point.

The styles adopted by Markham in his letters, and by Helen in her journal, are very noticeably different. Markham is not a reflective character, and his racy, conversational letters are chiefly concerned with the mystery of the Hall, the village gossip, life at home with his mother, his farm, and country parties. His own growing passion for Helen is at the centre of his thoughts, but he describes rather than reflects upon it. His portrait of life in a country village, suddenly surprised by an unexpected arrival, almost lives and breathes. Helen's journal, on the other hand, is most vivid when she is writing about her inner thoughts and feelings. The world she inhabits with Huntingdon is in dramatic contrast to Markham's, but she does not bring it to life with the same enlivening touch. Grassdale Manor and its landscape remain hazy (except when it is described under snow – by Markham), while Markham's description of Wildfell Hall, beginning 'Silent and grim it frowned before us' (Chapter 6), sets it immediately before the eye. Many of the major characters in Helen's world, such as Millicent or Walter, remain ill-defined, and the conversation, even for such an artificial society, is often grotesquely stilted. Huntingdon himself is frighteningly brought to life, and so are many of the scenes of drunken violence, but Helen's skill lies more in conveying her own fortitude, disillusion, and disgust. Her frequent use of biblical language emphasises the serious, moral nature of her writing. Whether this difference between her writing and Markham's is deliberate, or whether it arose because Anne was familiar with village life and unfamiliar with the drawing-rooms of the wealthy and debauched, we can never be sure. But, like her sisters, she was a very conscious artist, and it is probable she knew precisely what she was doing.

The imagery falls naturally and easily, without emphasis, and is much sparser than in the writing of her sisters. Sometimes it is harsh and vivid, as in the whipping of Lawrence, or Lowborough's burning of Hattersley's hand; sometimes (in the manner of all the Brontës) it is inspired by landscape or weather. The description of the sea beginning, 'the blue sea burst upon our sight' (Chapter 7) is as lively as Agnes's at the end of *Agnes Grey*. Symbolic scenes are not frequent in Anne's work, but Helen's presentation of the winter rose is a touching symbolic gesture, saved from sentimentality by Markham's initial failure to understand it.

Characters

Helen Huntingdon/Markham: Helen begins her adult life with no more sense than any other girl swept off her feet by glittering balls and handsome young men. Her destiny is to win her way through to humility and wisdom by harsh experience. The reader first meets her through Markham's description of her charm and intelligence. Her independence and her talents become plain as the Markhams begin to know her. The intriguing mystery which surrounds her and her young son is not explained until she gives Markham her journal, and only then does the reader begin to understand her story. She was dazzled by Huntingdon when she first met him in London, and in her pride was full of confidence that she could reform his wild life. She becomes infatuated, jealous, and full of excuses for his behaviour, which she believes arises from 'his joyous, playful spirit'. But after marriage she soon begins to see how useless are her hopes of reform; Huntingdon is selfish, bullying, drunken, and depraved. But Helen's courage sustains her, and her sense of wifely duty, as well as her devotion to her son, keep her at Grassdale until Huntingdon's conduct becomes so intolerable she feels justified in leaving him. Her courage carries her through her secret departure for Wildfell Hall, even though she has already been once discovered in her plan, and robbed of all her money and jewels.

She is determined to keep her son, and to rescue him from his father's attempts to 'make a man of him'. Even when Huntingdon is dying, she makes him promise that she is to be the boy's sole protector. Her horror of drink has become so deep that she gives the boy an emetic to make him dislike it. Her departure from her husband did not mean that she had abandoned the contract of marriage; she tells Markham that perhaps they will never be together, and she later returns to nurse her husband, not only from duty but from pity. She is a compassionate woman, who longs for some glimmer of repentance from him, so that he will be assured of heaven. And she believes that even when she finds no remorse, he will ultimately find forgiveness. She is compassionate towards the Hattersleys, and to the miseries of Lowborough. Lowborough's marriage is an interesting reverse of her own; as she deludes herself that she can reform Huntingdon, so he deludes himself that Annabella can reform him.

In spite of her despair, she resists the offered love and help of Hargrave. Her love for Markham grows slowly but steadily, and when he does not write she believes that she has lost him. It is only through her enterprise in inviting him in at Stanningley, and offering the rose, that he is able to overcome the barrier of her wealth and ask her to marry him. Like all Brontë heroines, she will accept no barriers to true love –

'the greatest worldly distinctions and discrepancies of rank, birth, and fortune are as dust in the balance compared with . . . truly loving, sympathising hearts and souls'.

Arthur Huntingdon: Apart from his looks, and a certain boisterous good-humour in youth, there is little to be said for Huntingdon. His pleasures are entirely selfish, and he behaves almost from the beginning as a libertine and a drunkard. He deliberately provokes Helen's jealousy by his flirtation with Annabella, taunts her with his search for other women, and in his rage at her refusal to cringe before him he offers her to his friends. He is jealous of the affection between Helen and his son, and attempts to corrupt the boy with swearing and drink, partly for his own amusement and partly to distress his wife. His installation of his mistress as Arthur's governess finally convinces Helen that she must leave.

In his last illness he becomes abjectly terrified of death, but when he is recovering he relapses again into obstinate, wilful drinking. The prospect of death makes him no kinder to Helen, whom he abuses even while he whines and clings. His character is seen only through the eyes of the much-abused Helen, and sometimes the portrait seems a little overdone, even verging on caricature. It is always possible that the author, in her determination to emphasise the evils of drink, had her eyes more on the message than on the character.

Gilbert Markham: Although we have no description of him, this prosperous young farmer is clearly handsome and attractive. The village girls, as well as Helen, find him pleasing, even though he is not altogether kind to Eliza. He is a cheerful son and brother, and as the writer of some half of the book he is observant, lively, and interested in all about him. His fascination with the mysterious tenant of the Hall soon grows into a passion, and his eavesdropping leads to suspicions of Lawrence which bring about the ugly scene of the horse-whipping. Like many Brontë men, he conceals traces of violence beneath a good-humoured exterior. He is energetic, active, and impatient, especially when he is travelling at speed to find Helen in the snow, and he shows little gentleness in his manner.

Once he has read Helen's journal he accepts with courage her refusal to promise herself, and he does not press her. After she has left the Hall, Lawrence gives him the news of her return to Huntingdon, which he finds almost impossible to bear. He longs for Huntingdon's death, but struggles to behave well. When Huntingdon does eventually die, Gilbert's pride, arising from his inferiority in wealth and rank, prevents him from rushing to Helen. It is only the terrible news of her imminent marriage which sends him off on his anguished snowy journey, and eventually to Stanningley. But his diffidence is such that he does not dare enter the house. When he is inside he is slow to believe that Helen loves and wishes to marry him.

Other characters: The novel includes a wide, rich range of characters, families, and couples, both in Markham's humble village and in Huntingdon's wealthy, idle circle. Some, such as Lawrence, Hattersley and Millicent, are awkward, without much breath of life. But others, such as the Markham family and the Lowboroughs, are complex, credible beings. On the whole, the people of the village (Mrs Markham, Rose and Fergus, the Millwards) are more sharply drawn than Huntingdon's friends, but they are less significant for the progress of the story. The portrait of the Rev. Millward, with his 'massive-featured face' mocks all pompous clerics with high-spirited irony.

The Hargrave family are used with the clear intention of illustrating various attitudes to marriage and to women. Mrs Hargrave wishes only that her daughters should make wealthy marriages, and become obedient wives. Millicent obliges by marrying the wealthy Hattersley, and deferring and cringing to him in a way Helen could never adopt to Huntingdon. The spirited Esther, however, reflects sadly on the position of unmarried women, yet refuses to marry except for love. Walter, who appears intelligent and kind, becomes a friend to Helen but wrecks his value in her eyes by trying to make her his mistress.

The handsome Annabella is a heartless flirt, who marries Lowborough for money and title, and causes him and Helen much grief. Yet she is vivacious, and her conversation has a genuine liveliness and wit which is too often lacking elsewhere in her circle. Her husband's character is interesting in that it alters and develops with experience. His naive belief in Annabella is shattered by her affair with Huntingdon, but with Helen's help he learns to deny himself drink, and eventually remarries sensibly and happily.

The faithful Rachel, devoted to Helen, is an elderly servant of sterling character, such as one learns to recognise in Brontë novels. She is stern in manner, and speaks in harsh, pithy sentences, but she is loving and loyal, and always on the watch for threat to her mistress.

Bibliography

The Brontës

ALLOTT, M. (ED.): *The Brontës: the critical heritage*, Routledge and Kegan Paul, London, 1974. A useful collection of essays, largely of the nineteenth century.

BENTLEY, P.: *The Brontës and their World*, Thames and Hudson, London, 1969. A brief text, but very fully illustrated with contemporary drawings and paintings.

DAVIES, S. (ED.): *The Brontë Sisters: selected poems*, Carcenet Press, London, 1976. A good, brief introduction and selection.

EAGLETON, T.: *Myths of Power: a Marxist study of the Brontës*, Macmillan, London, 1975. A fresh, controversial interpretation.

GREGOR, I. (ED.): *The Brontës: a collection of critical essays*, Prentice-Hall, New York, 1970. Good twentieth-century criticism, complementing Allott (see above).

PINION, F.B.: *A Brontë Companion*, Macmillan, London, 1975. An invaluable collection of facts, comments, and literary interpretation.

RATCHFORD, F.E.: *The Brontës' Web of Childhood*, Columbia University Press, New Jersey, 1941, rev. 1964. A study and interpretation of the youthful writings.

SPARK, M. (ED.): *The Brontë Letters: a selection*, Peter Owen, London, 1954.

WINNIFRITH, T.: *The Brontës*, Macmillan, London, 1977. A lively general account of their lives and works.

Charlotte Brontë

WORKS

The Professor: JACK, J. AND SMITH, M. (EDS), Clarendon Press, Oxford, 1967.

Jane Eyre: JACK, J. AND SMITH, M. (EDS), Clarendon Press, Oxford, 1969.

—: LANE, M. (Introduction), Everyman, Dent, London, 1983.

—: LEAVIS, Q.D. (Introduction and Notes), Penguin English Library, Harmondsworth, 1966.

—: SMITH, M. (ED.), World's Classics, Oxford University Press, London, 1980.
There are also innumerable other editions.
Shirley: HOOK, A. AND HOOK, J. (EDS), Penguin English Library, Harmondsworth, 1974.
—: ROSENGARTEN, H. AND SMITH, M. (EDS), Clarendon Press, Oxford, 1979.
—: ROSENGARTEN, H. (ED.), World's Classics, Oxford University Press, London, 1981.
Villette: DRABBLE, M. (Introduction), Everyman, Dent, London, 1983.
—: ROSENGARTEN, H. AND SMITH, M. (EDS), Clarendon Press, Oxford, 1985.
—: TANNER, T. (ED.), Penguin English Library, Harmondsworth, 1979.

BIOGRAPHY AND CRITICISM

ALLOTT, M. (ED.), *Jane Eyre and Villette: a casebook*, Macmillan, London, 1973. Reviews and essays.
GASKELL, MRS E.: *The Life of Charlotte Brontë* (first published 1857), introduction by M. Lane, Everyman, Dent, London, 1960.
Also ed. A. Shelston, Penguin English Library, Harmondsworth, 1975.
GÉRIN, W.: *Charlotte Brontë, the Evolution of Genius*, Clarendon Press, Oxford, 1967. The standard biography.
LANE, M.: *The Brontë Story: a reconstruction of Mrs Gaskell's 'Life'*, Heinemann, London, 1953. Provides many new insights and corrections.
MOGLEN, H.: *Charlotte Brontë*, Norton, New York, 1976. Not an easy book, but an excellent study.

Emily Brontë

WORKS

Wuthering Heights: DAICHES, D. (ED.), Penguin English Library, Harmondsworth, 1970.
—: JACK, I. AND MARSDEN, H. (EDS), Clarendon Press, Oxford, 1976.
—: JACK, I. (ED.), World's Classics, Oxford University Press, London, 1981.
—: KER WILSON, B. (Introduction), together with some of the poems, Blackie, London, 1979.
Poems: HATFIELD, C.W. (ED.), Clarendon Press, Oxford, 1941.

BIOGRAPHY AND CRITICISM

ALLOTT, M. (ED.), *Emily Brontë: a casebook*, Macmillan, London, 1970. Reviews and essays.

GÉRIN, W.: *Emily Brontë, a biography*, Clarendon Press, Oxford, 1971, new edn, Oxford University Press, London, 1978.

SMITH, A. (ED.): *The Art of Emily Brontë*, Vision Press, London, 1976. Stimulating essays by various hands.

SPARK, M. AND STANFORD, D.: *Emily Brontë, her life and work*, Peter Owen, London, 1953; a new edn, 1975. A readable and lively account.

Anne Brontë

WORKS

The Clarendon Press editions of Anne Brontë's novels have not yet appeared.

Agnes Grey: Everyman, Dent, London, 1984.

The Tenant of Wildfell Hall: HARGREAVES, D.G. (ED.), Introduction W.Gérin, Penguin English Library, Harmondsworth, 1979.

BIOGRAPHY AND CRITICISM

GÉRIN, W.: *Anne Brontë*, Nelson, London, 1959; new edn, Allen Lane, Penguin Books, London 1976.

SCOTT, P.M.J.: *Anne Brontë: a new critical assessment*, Vision Press, London, 1983. An enthusiastic and persuasive plea for recognition.

Index

The index should be used in conjunction with the Table of Contents (p.3). The abbreviation 'cha.' denotes a character-description.

Further titles

THE ENGLISH NOVEL
IAN MILLIGAN

This Handbook deals with the English novel from the historical, thematic and technical points of view, and discusses the various purposes of authors and the manner in which they achieve their effects, as well as the role of the reader. The aim is to bring to light the variety of options at the novelist's disposal and to enhance the reader's critical and interpretive skills – and pleasure.

Ian Milligan is Lecturer in English at the University of Stirling.

A DICTIONARY OF LITERARY TERMS
MARTIN GRAY

Over one thousand literary terms are dealt with in this Handbook, with definitions, explanations and examples. Entries range from general topics (comedy, epic, metre, romanticism) to more specific terms (acrostic, enjambment, malapropism, onomatopoeia) and specialist technical language (catalexis, deconstruction, *haiku*, paeon). In other words, this single, concise volume should meet the needs of anyone searching for clarification of terms found in the study of literature.

Martin Gray is Lecturer in English at the University of Stirling.

AN INTRODUCTION TO LITERARY CRITICISM
RICHARD DUTTON

This is an introduction to a subject that has received increasing emphasis in the study of literature in recent years. As a means of identifying the underlying principles of the subject, the author examines the way in which successive eras and individual critics have applied different yardsticks by which to judge literary output. In this way the complexities of modern criticism are set in the perspective of its antecedents, and seen as only the most recent links in a chain of changing outlooks and methods of approach. The threads of this analysis are drawn together in the concluding chapter, which offers a blueprint for the practice of criticism.

Richard Dutton is Lecturer in English Literature at the University of Lancaster.

STUDYING CHAUCER
ELISABETH BREWER

STUDYING SHAKESPEARE
MARTIN STEPHEN and PHILIP FRANKS

STUDYING MILTON
GEOFFREY M. RIDDEN

STUDYING CHARLES DICKENS
K. J. FIELDING

STUDYING THOMAS HARDY
LANCE ST JOHN BUTLER

AN A·B·C OF SHAKESPEARE
P. C. BAYLEY

ENGLISH LITERATURE FROM THE THIRD WORLD
TREVOR JAMES

EFFECTIVE STUDYING
STEVE ROBERTSON and DAVID SMITH

AN INTRODUCTORY GUIDE TO ENGLISH LITERATURE
MARTIN STEPHEN

PREPARING FOR EXAMINATIONS IN ENGLISH LITERATURE
NEIL McEWAN

ENGLISH POETRY
CLIVE T. PROBYN

ENGLISH USAGE
COLIN G. HEY

ENGLISH GRAMMAR
LORETO TODD

STYLE IN ENGLISH PROSE
NEIL McEWAN

READING THE SCREEN
An Introduction to Film Studies
JOHN IZOD

The author of this Handbook

SHEILA SULLIVAN is a graduate in English of the University of Oxford and holds a Diploma in Psychology, University of London. She has worked at the Oxford University Press; taught English for several years; edited *Critics on Chaucer* (1970) and *Critics on T.S. Eliot* (1973); contributed to *The Genius of Thomas Hardy* (1976); and worked for three years as an assistant editor and writer on the new *Oxford Companion to English Literature*. She has recently published a long introduction on T.S. Eliot to Victor Purcell's *The Sweeniad*, and is the author of York Notes on Laurence Sterne's *A Sentimental Journey*.